THERAPEUTIC FRIENDSHIP

Smyth & Helwys Publishing, Inc.
6316 Peake Road
Macon, Georgia 31210-3960
1-800-747-3016

Library of Congress Cataloging-in-Publication Data

Names: O'Rear, Christopher D., author.
Title: Therapeutic friendship : cultivating relationships that heal / by
Christopher D. O'Rear.
Description: Macon, GA : Smyth & Helwys Publishing, 2024. | Includes
bibliographical references.
Identifiers: LCCN 2024026682 | ISBN 9781641735759 (paperback)
Subjects: LCSH: Friendship--Religious aspects--Christianity. |
Counseling--Religious aspects--Christianity. | Pastoral counseling.
Classification: LCC BV4647.F7 O74 2024 | DDC 241/.6762--dc23/eng/20240628
LC record available at https://lccn.loc.gov/2024026682

CHRISTOPHER D. O'REAR

THERAPEUTIC FRIENDSHIP

Cultivating Relationships that Heal

Advance Praise for *Therapeutic Friendship*

To the volume of books written to help humans navigate relationships, this book is a wonderful addition. With the training of a therapist and the honesty of one who has learned from his own life, Chris O'Rear offers layers and layers of practical wisdom for how we can relate, grow, and continue to learn from being in community with others. Along the way he offers a rich glimpse of additional material available for how to avoid pitfalls and step toward greater wholeness for everyone.

—Judy Skeen
Professor of Religion, Belmont University
Courage & Renewal facilitator, spiritual director

In a refreshingly straightforward and candid manner, Chris O'Rear draws upon his experience as a pastoral psychotherapist to teach us how to form relationships that heal instead of hurt. His words are both practical and wise. Whether you want to be a better therapist, friend, or family member, this book will be a resource you turn to again and again. Highly recommended!

—Bruce Rogers-Vaughn
Associate Professor, Practice of Pastoral Theology
and Counseling Vanderbilt Divinity School (retired)
Author of Caring for Souls in a Neoliberal Age

"What I look for in a book are the same things I look for in a therapist or a friend: wisdom, honesty, and bravery, in league with vulnerability, humility, and love. This book has all these qualities, as does Chris O'Rear himself. I'll be a better therapist—and a better friend—for having read it."

—Russell Siler Jones
Psychotherapist and author of Spirit in Session

With genuine authenticity, gleaning on his professional, clinical, and personal experience, Chris offers a solid framework for developing our "emotional toolbox," inviting us to discover the transformational nature of deep and meaningful relationships. As we strive toward the goal of emotional health, good and healthy relationships with both clinicians and friends help us embrace ourselves to the fullest. In doing so, we become agents of God's presence and love for others, as we experience God's love for us through them. Reminding us that it's about "progress, not perfection," Chris's words invited me into a safe and sacred space of rediscovering the therapeutic quality of good and healthy friendships.

—Rev. Renée Lloyd Owen, MDiv
Endorser & Director of Chaplaincy & Pastoral Counseling Ministries
Cooperative Baptist Fellowship

I have been learning from Chris for years, as both friend and fellow church member. He really does embody the "humble curiosity" described in this book. Readers will understand, as I have witnessed in person, how a professional's experience can mix with a life well lived to yield tremendous insight and care.

—Cliff Vaughn
Media Producer, Good Faith Media

This book is dedicated to my wife, Lynda, who has been my partner, spouse, and best friend on the roller coaster of life.

Acknowledgments

This book would not exist if it were not for the friendship of my many "lunch friends," lifelong friends, mentors, colleagues, and coworkers, especially Steve Gillespie. Steve's continuing education presentation on friendship many years ago first inspired me to think about the concepts presented in this book. He also gave me the gift of being a kind and supportive friend and coworker at the Pastoral Counseling Centers of Tennessee, Inc. Many friends have shaped me over the years, and many of them are described throughout the book. I am grateful for my friends who helped bring this project to fruition through encouraging me, reading early drafts, and offering feedback. I am grateful for the imprint that each friendship has left on my life.

Contents

Introduction

The lyrics of the old hymn by Scriven and Crozat remind us, "What a friend we have in Jesus" (1885). However, it has been my experience that we often experience the friendship of Jesus through the presence of a friend or loved one who embodies the ideals of God's love for us, whether at a specific moment or through steadfast presence over time. It seems, then, to be equally accurate to assert, "What a Jesus we have in friends." Most of my own theological development of the last twenty-eight years began with a moment for me when the presence of a friend was transformational. I have more understanding of that event and its context at this point in my life than I did when it happened, but it literally changed the trajectory of my life.

My development of faith was complicated, and I have heard from friends that I can sometimes be hard on my younger self. As a young person, I carried a great burden of responsibility for others, and I experienced the burden as an extension of my faith. The development of my faith was greatly influenced by the experiences of my childhood family and the churches that we attended throughout my growing years. I look back on my younger self and remember being more perfectionistic, self-righteous, and driven by rule keeping. When I say these things, friends respond that I can be too hard on myself, but I know that whether I wore it on the outside or simply carried it as an internal attitude, I did not feel that there was room for me to step outside the expected behaviors and patterns, and I did take pride in keeping the rules. I was an overachiever, president of the student body, voted "Best All-Around" in high school; I felt like I had no choice but to be a rule-keeping achiever. Success and achievement only reinforced the need for more success and achievement. The drive was fueled by insecurity and a need for affirmation that pushed me to get more affirmation.

My parents divorced when I was twenty-five years old, and that change was very difficult for me. I did not realize how much of my identity and faith was wrapped up in my family role, but when my parents divorced, I felt like God had failed me. I felt that I had failed my family, and I lost my sense of who I was. It did not help that at this same time my dreams of being a doctor were finally put to rest when I was not accepted to medical school for the second time. To be honest, "the dream" of going to medical school had died years before, but I had not been able to admit that to anyone, including myself. I began seminary then without clarity of purpose, but professional ministry was the only other profession I had ever felt called to.

While I was in seminary, one of my professors recommended that I begin counseling after I shared my thoughts and emotions stirred by my parents' divorce. I learned that the seminary would help pay for the first several sessions of counseling. In that early therapy, I began to learn about the various influences and internal narratives that had shaped me, and I began to reflect on the level of duty and responsibility that I carried. By the time I was thirty, I had come to a place in my life where I began to question many decisions, including my own marriage. I was weary of living out of duty and responsibility. At the time, I did not have the capacity or insight to fully articulate these thoughts, and my expression of them was unsophisticated and reactionary. I began to make changes in my life not with a well-conceived strategy but with an emotionally driven reactionary attempt to free myself from what felt confining. I see now that this was a blind striving to find freedom and become an authentic self. I just had no idea what that meant, and I certainly did not use that language at the time. To those outside, it just seemed that I was spinning out of control like the Looney Tunes Tasmanian Devil, wreaking havoc and causing destruction for pretty much everyone in my life.

My wife and I separated for a while during this time. Family and other people would tell me things like, "You know what the right thing to do is; just do the right thing." I knew I was tired of doing the right thing for the right thing's sake, but I was overwhelmed with guilt. Because I was no longer living into the expectations of others, I felt like I was not lovable as I was, and I behaved in ways that were quite selfish. I felt rejected and unloved but did not want to take again the yoke of responsibility and perfectionism. I did not feel capable of returning to life as it had been, I did not like where I was, and I was not sure what the future was supposed to be. I was miserable and felt like the prodigal son eating with the pigs he was feeding (Luke 15:11-24). In that time of feeling unloved and unlovable, I got a phone call from a friend, Mike Lature.[1] Mike had been a good friend for several years. He had heard a bit of my story and called me one evening to ask what was going on. I did not have the awareness to offer him a good explanation of my feelings but stumbled over my words as best I could. I still sounded selfish and unrepentant. Mike listened to me, asked questions, and then he said, "I don't really understand all that you are saying, but I know this: you are my friend, I love you, and you will always be my friend." Something in Mike's words hit me hard. I did not feel loveable, but he professed his love for me. As I sat with his words, I began to cry. The crying became heaving sobs, and I cried for what seemed like hours.

Mike backed up his statement by coming to me where I lived in another state and helping move my few belongings back to Tennessee, where another lifelong friend, Lyn Robbins, and his family offered me a place to stay for a while. Through some good therapy and marriage counseling, I began to grow in understanding myself. My wife and I reconciled and have currently been married for thirty-seven years. I deeply regret the events that I went through and the pain I caused Lynda, our friends, and my family. I also know that through those events, I came to a place where I was able to affirm that I chose Lynda not out of obligation but because she was the best person for me. We have been steadfast friends and partners since that time. We recently reflected on how we have "grown up together" over the years, emotionally speaking, and how good things seem to be for us these days. I have learned to be a more authentic and open version of myself. I have learned to let go of the need to be perfect and to have patience with myself. This, in turn, has made me

---

1. When full names are used throughout the book, they are used with permission. Names and identifying information for others have been altered to protect those identities.

more patient with others. I have learned to deal with life as it comes without being angry when life is not what I expect it to be. One of the biggest changes from that earlier time is the shift in my understanding of God.

A part of me dramatically changed the night of my friend's phone call. I had been at one of the lowest points of my life. I struggled with my identity, the meaning of my existence, and, at times, if existence was even desirable. My friend's love for me as I was at that moment was disorienting but deeply meaningful. The love of God that I had professed earlier in my life took on new meaning in my friend's words and the acts of kindness shown over the next several months. The day after that profound moment on the phone with my friend Mike, though, I woke up and my life was still a mess. I still was not sure what needed to happen. It would take years for me to work through it all, and I had a lot to learn about myself and others. Many significant events, people, and experiences helped in my transformation, but they all began with that one phone call from my friend that set me on a new trajectory. The love I experienced in Mike began to shift my thinking, my theology, and my life.

I was baptized at the age of seven and had talked about the love of God for years, but I finally had a profound experience of God's love that was transformational. I began to try to understand how I could live out that love in every part of my life and in every relationship. I began to reread the Bible through a new lens. I began to seek friends and sought to be a friend who would embody God's love, which my friends had embodied for me. I would later have experiences in psychotherapy that helped me better understand myself. I learned how good psychotherapy can embody this theological understanding and how the presence of a good therapist or friend can embody God's presence in my life.

This book is a collection of thoughts and reflections from my own study, my training as a psychotherapist, my experience in providing psychotherapy for others, and my experience with my friends over the years. It also grows out of my personal experience of being a client in psychotherapy and being nurtured by several wonderful therapists and one amazing psychoanalyst. (I will say more about the various types of therapy below.) I believe that good and healthy friendships can have a therapeutic quality. I want to be clear, however, that while friendship can be therapeutic, friendship is not a substitute for a process of good, self-reflective psychotherapy. I believe that both psychotherapy and deep friendships can be spiritual experiences that lead to growth and self-understanding, but one is not a substitute for the other. Friendships can be a support for us, can help us stay grounded, process feelings, feel connected, and challenge us.

Psychotherapy helps us explore issues of growth and development affected by our family of origin and history. It can help us identify and overcome unconscious or semiconscious motives that are unproductive. It can help us identify and process traumatic events and learn better coping strategies. Psychotherapy can help us grow in self-awareness, work on changing things that can be changed and make peace with things that cannot be changed. It can help us identify ways to deepen our relationships with others through better expression of our feelings and healthier communication. Friendship can be a great laboratory to identify issues to take to therapy and to practice things that we learn in therapy. All these things are important for a meaningful life.

In this book, I will share thoughts on why our common ideas of friendship are sometimes inadequate for meeting our needs. This will help us understand why even though we might have many "friends," we persist in feeling lonely. Many of the listening and caring skills that I have learned as a psychotherapist and experienced as a psychotherapy client can be adapted and utilized to help deepen our connections with other people. Raising awareness of these skills and dynamics can also bring us closer to loving ourselves and loving our neighbor in a way that does not feel burdensome but brings meaning and joy. I want to look at the qualities and characteristics of friendship that cultivate deep, meaningful, transformative connections. Having even one or two people in our lives with whom we have a deeper connection can help us feel more grounded, less anxious, and more aware of ourselves.

Good friends sometimes have misunderstandings and disagreements. We can be hurt, and we can hurt others, usually unintentionally.

Having occasional misunderstandings and hurt feelings is not a sign of relationships ending but an indicator that a relationship needs attention. Having tools to deal with hurt relationships is important, and navigating such difficulties can often lead to a deepening of the relationship and a better understanding of ourselves. A good friend can help us grow, help shape our ideas of who God is, and may even be the voice of God for us from time to time. I hope this book will help you grow in awareness of yourself. I hope you develop skills and attitudes that will cultivate deep relationships in which you can be the presence of God for others and experience God in others.

I want to explain my use of the word "psychotherapy" in this book. I will share some of the technical differences in types of counseling and psychotherapy in later chapters; however, in my early experiences of being a client in counseling, I participated in both psychotherapy and psychoanalysis. The psychotherapy was "psychodynamic" or "insight-oriented" in nature. This type of therapy is related to a process of psychoanalysis initially developed by Sigmund Freud and modified by others through the years. (I will say more about psychoanalysis later.)

Psychodynamic psychotherapy is oriented to assisting clients in understanding their own internal world. Using the client's report of any interaction with another person, from mundane to dramatic; the client's report of their internal thoughts, fears, and feelings; and the client's dreams or fantasies, the therapist assists the client in improving self-awareness. It is true that understanding the internal world does not automatically create change in a person, but understanding the internal world provides an opportunity to make strategic change. A good process of psychotherapy can help a person better understand why they behave the way they do in given situations. It can help them feel more comfortable with thoughts and feelings that might initially upset or confuse them. Good psychotherapy can utilize growth and understanding to help a client change how they relate to others through education that helps overcome past beliefs, behaviors, and interactions. Once a person gains this knowledge and ability, they are more likely to continue to apply their new awareness and learning to novel situations. This type of psychodynamic or psychoanalytic psychotherapy was truly transformational for me and offered a path to emotional, mental, relational, and spiritual renewal.

Much of what is taught in schools of clinical counseling today is driven by factors other than a desire for client transformation. Current counseling methods are more oriented toward evaluating symptoms and applying specified techniques that are shown to be effective (at least in the short term) in reducing the presenting symptoms. This is a "medical model" of counseling. However, emotional, mental, relational, and spiritual health is not like a broken arm or a respiratory illness. There is not a one-size-fits-all treatment. As much as pharmaceutical companies would like us to believe otherwise, there is also no pill that will resolve all our internal conflicts, historical wounds, and complicated personality issues. To be clear, I am not opposed to the use of medication as part of a treatment plan for a person when it is needed. But no medication will completely eliminate the need for the personal work of introspection and change.

When I talk about the benefits of psychotherapy and reference how friendship can mirror psychotherapy, I am talking about insight-oriented, psychodynamic psychotherapy designed to deepen a person's self-understanding and sense of well-being. It is not an easy process and rarely occurs through short-term therapy. I hope this book will help clarify these dynamics, make them more accessible for you in everyday life, and help reduce general misconceptions about the process of therapy.

Chapter 1

Hiding & Being Known

People sometimes discuss whether the first man and first woman of the Bible were literal people. In my reflections, whether they were literal people or not, their story serves as a representation of the individual developmental journeys of each of us and of all kinds of relationships. Before Adam and Eve ate of the fruit and gained the knowledge of good and evil, the Bible describes them as naked and unashamed (Gen 2:25). This nakedness could be understood as symbolic as well as literal. They did not have coverings on their bodies, and that allowed them to be physically seen and known. They did not fear the reaction of the other, and they were able to be exposed without concern of rejection or ridicule. Once they ate the fruit, the first thing they did was cover their bodies and hide. In an ideal relational state, we are fully seen and loved for who we are, not necessarily despite who we are but because of who we are. In ideal intimate long-term romantic relationships, the partners see each other fully naked physically but also live and share with each other to the point that they are known fully emotionally, intellectually, and spiritually. The regular acceptance of one partner or spouse by the other is an affirmation of that person and creates emotional safety that allows one to feel grounded, connected, and loved. This is perhaps a reason that the marital relationship and sexual love is sometimes used in the Bible as a metaphor for God's love for us.

Platonic friendships are typically defined as having a level of emotional closeness without the physical or sexual aspects of a romantic relationship. Good friends should have the experience of knowing each other intimately and still choosing the friendship. When another person knows our idiosyncrasies, fears, dreams, frailties, and strengths and still desires to spend time with us and continues to love us, we feel valued, safe, and grounded. This connection with another is one of the biggest antidotes to loneliness—perhaps *the* antidote. However, like the fallen Adam and Eve, most of us, in one way or another, seek to hide from each other, and our culture reinforces this by emphasizing our insecurity, playing on our fears, and creating ways for us to hide. Not only do we hide from others; we can also develop ways of hiding from ourselves. In a world where we fear rejection or injury by others, we seek to protect ourselves in a variety of ways.

We will look at several ways we defend ourselves in a future chapter, but one of the fundamental ways is by never letting ourselves be known in the first place. Many of us grow up in families or cultures that reject certain feelings, attitudes, or outlooks and praise or reinforce other ways of being. We learn, often through unspoken rules, that certain parts of ourselves are not acceptable, and we begin to hide these parts while emphasizing and presenting others more regularly. In a recent conversation I had with a client, she talked about her family and how certain topics were taboo subjects for conversation. She said, "It's not like anyone ever said don't talk about these things, but somehow we knew." This is how many families, churches, workplaces, or other groups operate. It is likely that no one ever says, "We will not talk about these things" or "These types of outlooks are not welcome," but somehow everyone in the system knows what those things are. Similarly, when a parent, a boss, or a leader never shows vulnerability, then those under them believe that vulnerability in such an environment (or any environment) is not safe or acceptable.

I heard of a pastor who preached a sermon in which he attempted to encourage people in their faith, but what he said could be paraphrased as, "You cannot be a true believer and have doubts." After receiving several notes and phone calls about this statement in the following week, the pastor tried to clarify his position the next Sunday by saying from the pulpit that of course people have doubts, and it is ok to have doubts. It would have been nice if he had stopped there, but apparently, he went on to add, "I have just never had doubts." I assume he intended this to somehow be comforting, but instead he negated his affirmation that doubts are acceptable. I do not imagine there were many people who sought out that pastor the next week to talk about the doubts they sometimes feel.

The idea that we must hide part of ourselves or that we only project what we believe to be acceptable has been referred to as a "false self" or a "mask." There are many books written about the development of a false self as a defensive strategy, but the bottom line is that most of us, to one degree or another, believe that if everything were known about us, we would not be acceptable. This fear is legitimized when we see various figures disgraced in the public after disclosure of some failing. So, if we have struggles, difficulties, or aspects of ourselves that we do not like, we tend to hide them from others. Instead, we choose to project to the world the aspects we think are more acceptable and make us look better. Whether this occurs at a conscious or unconscious level, the result is the same. Social media has only reinforced this idea and nurtured comparison, envy, competition, and emotional disconnect on platforms that are purported to create connection. However, whether online or in person, we can project a social self that keeps people from knowing us fully and protects us from the vulnerability of being fully known. If we are liked, we believe it is because people like the person we project to be, and this reinforces the belief that our true self should remain hidden.

I do not necessarily like the concept of a *false* self. This implies that the image we show to others is not real, genuine, or authentic. In some cases, this may be true. There are definitely people in the world who behave one way in public in order to maintain an image but are quite different people when out of the public view. There are those who are aware they are projecting a particular image and do so in order to control or manipulate others. There are also those who become so invested in the image they show the world that they begin to believe the image is who they truly are. Such people can become defensive or angry when anything is said or done that might imply that they are not the person that they project to the world. The idea that they might have what they perceive as faults or flaws is so unacceptable that they would rather reject the person who brings such things to light rather than acknowledge or deal with issues when they arise. Such people have difficulty admitting when they are wrong and often have a need to always be right. The public image is a "false self" because it does not acknowledge the totality of the person.

However, what most of us do, consciously or semiconsciously, is simply show the parts of ourselves that we feel are most acceptable or least objectionable. It is not *false* in the sense that it is fake or fraudulent. It is, however, carefully crafted to hide the aspects of ourselves that we do not like or do not believe would be acceptable. Doing this allows a sense of safety within our social groups and society as a whole.

Another aspect of this attempt to maintain a sense of safety involves limiting our association with others to those we believe are like us. We tend to feel safer being fully ourselves when surrounded by people we perceive to be like us. If the people around us talk like us and share our views, etc., then we feel safer sharing our views and values because we see them reflected to us from the group. Others who are not the same become suspect or are rejected because we perceive them as unsafe. We do this in many ways, but it generally involves reducing other people to some aspect of themselves and rejecting them based on that one quality or characteristic. This is evident in the language we use and the labels we apply to others. We divide ourselves by nationality, skin color, religion, socioeconomic status, sexual preference, and more. We might divide the world by labels like gay or straight, Democrat or Republican, Southern or Northern, old or young, and on and on. Any time we observe *us* and *them* language creeping into our vocabulary, we know that we are potentially guilty of reducing the other to something less than human. Phrases like "*Those people* do this" or "*They* are like that" can reveal our biases. Surrounding ourselves with people like us is a way to create the illusion of social safety, but it is an illusion because freedom to be ourselves begins within ourselves.

The part of ourselves that we keep hidden from others is often something that we also disown or dislike in ourselves. Psychoanalyst Carl Jung and Jungian analysts refer to these aspects as our "shadow." In his book, *Make Friends with Your Shadow: How to Accept and Use Positively the Negative Side of Your Personality*, William Miller describes how maintaining our shadow side begins to affect us negatively. The

denied parts of ourselves will often find unconscious expression in
ways that create difficulty for us. If we understand these parts, learn
to "make friends" with them, and understand the needs they represent, we can choose to express them in constructive ways. Apart from
this acceptance, aspects of our personality have a tendency, as I say,
to "squeeze out sideways," often in ways that are hurtful to us and
reinforce our feelings of shame about them.

Our shadow side is also problematic because it requires mental
and emotional energy to continue denying it within ourselves and
keeping it hidden from others. In order to do so, we may draw
boundaries around topics and issues that might lead us to disclose or
acknowledge these parts of ourselves. We keep people at an emotional
distance to avoid anyone getting close enough to know us well. This
is one of the reasons that maintaining relationships with people like
us feels safer. If we are drawn to people who are also well defended
and only share things that feel safe, then we have created the illusion
of safety, but we do not experience the deep connection of vulnerability and authenticity. Our relationships only serve to perpetuate
our loneliness.

The world of social media has exacerbated this dynamic, as people
create posts that reflect the ideal parts of their lives. We might be
tempted to look at them and wonder why our lives are not as great,
but we do not see what exists outside the images and comments. We
do not know what is going on in every aspect of a person's life. Sure,
we all have some friends who seem to have it all together, but the
reality is that no one is perfect, and no one has it *all* together. The
Twelve Step recovery tradition advises, "Don't judge your insides by
looking at someone else's outside."

In the social media world, we can also be tempted to easily sort
ourselves and others into homogenous groups. We join the Facebook
group promoting certain beliefs or causes. Some people write hateful
comments on posts made by people with differing views. We reject
what is not like us and surround ourselves with people who seem
to be like us. This creates an illusion of emotional safety where we
believe that we are "free to be ourselves," but the self we are being is
limited and the connections we make are limited. We may end up

feeling lonely and depressed if we are not mindful of this and seeking to make deeper connections with others around us.

Kyle & Me

Several years ago, I was assigned to teach a Sunday school class at church with a fellow member named Kyle Cantrell. Kyle worked at a local radio station. He and I had been in a Sunday school class together previously, and based on that experience, I felt confident that Kyle and I did not share much in common regarding theological understanding or political affiliation. Often, I was astonished by things Kyle said because they were so different from my own views and values. It seemed symbolic that we sat on opposite sides of our classroom. However, Kyle and I were eventually asked to co-teach a college Sunday school class. Based on my limited experience with Kyle, I was concerned about how we would manage the task of teaching together. One Sunday, Kyle suggested we go to lunch together. I politely agreed, and the date was set. I was a bit apprehensive but felt confident that lunch would be ok, and I would at least enjoy a good meal.

As Kyle and I talked over lunch, we discovered a common love of music. I found that Kyle had an encyclopedic knowledge of classic country music and that music had served us each well as a "friend" through various times in our lives. Kyle and I shared similar anxieties about being a husband and a father. We shared our spiritual journeys, and I learned how Kyle saw his work in radio as part of a larger ministry to the community that went well beyond playing music on air. We were at lunch for at least two hours and agreed to meet again soon. Over the next several years, Kyle and I met for lunch and shared about life, music, and faith. Kyle received what I shared with grace and love. We grew in respect for one another, and we even developed a community program titled "The World According to Country Music" that included clips of classic country songs, bits of information and trivia about the songs and artists, and reflection on the underlying beliefs, values, and theologies reflected in the music. We had the opportunity to share that program with several different groups. My friendship with Kyle was always kind of amazing to me because, based on labels and my comfort zone, we were not compatible. But he was way more than the labels I might have placed on him.

On the opposite side, I recall a man of some success with whom I visited years ago. One of the reasons he came to talk with me was for help with his feelings of emptiness and loneliness. One day I asked him, "Who in your life really knows you?" He looked at me with confusion, pondered my question, and replied, "There is no one in my life that I don't have to be *something* for." In other words, he felt that for every person in his life, he was only the role he served for that person. He was the boss, the provider, the helper, the fixer, and on and on. In each of those roles, he felt that no one knew him as a person, and he believed it was only the role that made him acceptable. I began to understand why he felt so lonely.

Types of Friends & Levels of Connection

In the broadest terms, we could define types of relationships as "Family," "Acquaintances," "Friends," and "Romantic Partners." These might overlap in a positive way: a person's romantic partner is also their best friend, or a person identifies a sibling or other family member as a friend. Because of the nature of each type of relationship and the expectations of each, some combinations can work, and others become problematic. Within the category of friendship, we can also delineate various levels of connection and meaning. However, my point here is that there are progressive levels of connection among people, and all these relationships have their place; the nature and quality of the relationship is what makes a difference and shapes us for good or ill.

Volumes have been written on the various relationships between family members. Family is a relationship that is fundamentally defined by the familial and generational connection between people. This connection is defined by genetics or choosing but is shaped by the roles of those in the family—parent, child, sibling, etc. Family relationships can be nurturing or hurtful and sometimes both. In the family we grow up in, we do not choose the people we are in a relationship with, and our connection is defined by their perceived role in our lives. Some people talk about the concept of "family of choice," and often this is a person or group of people with a close friendship that feels like a family should and can become like a family for those who, for whatever reason, may not have such relationships or may not be close to their biological families. The key concept is that friendships tend to be more about choice than about genetics.

Acquaintances

Within the category of friendship, we can identify levels of connection, and each represents a deepening of connection and responsibility for the well-being of the other. We refer to some people as "Acquaintances." These are people we know because of our participation in certain groups, institutions, or activities. These are the people we work with, go to school with, attend church with, or work out with at the gym. Sometimes we do not even know the full names of such people and only recognize them by their faces. We participate in shared activities and may talk about those things, but we don't often talk about more. Sometimes a group, like a Sunday school class or small group at church, might encourage sharing of a personal nature, but in many such groups, sharing is limited to what seems safest to share. We might share concern about a coworker undergoing cancer treatment but not our recent struggle for patience with our children or our battle with feelings of depression. So, even in groups where a deeper connection is encouraged, in the social arrangement of acquaintances, we keep things at a safer level. In this category, we might also include friends we see for a shared social purpose. For example, you and your friend from church might regularly go to a sporting event together, but you generally talk about your work, the shared context in which you met, or the team you are supporting at the event. These are good relationships, but they do not always have a great deal of depth. Many people are comfortable at this level because such relationships do not require much personal risk. We do not talk about deeper things or share our struggles; we simply spend time enjoying common interests. I want to be clear that these relationships are not bad at all, and they are not unimportant. Men, in particular, tend to make connections around shared activities, and having an outlet for common interests or hobbies is an important part of socialization and self-care. However, emotionally speaking, these relationships require less vulnerability from us and are not always our most deeply fulfilling relationships. It is also true that there may be friendships that include shared activities *and* a deeper level of connection.

Friendships

The next level of relationship is a bit more challenging. As relationships deepen, there is an increasing level of self-disclosure, a deepening of emotional vulnerability and connection, and a greater feeling of responsibility for one another. This deepening of connection does not automatically happen. Marissa Franco, in her book *Platonic*, observes that relationships that matter require initiative and do not happen organically. She notes that "believing friendships happen organically—that cosmic energies will bestow friends upon you—actually *hinders* people from making friends" (66–67). This kind of connection can sound like a blossoming romance because we are so accustomed to thinking about romantic relationships as our primary point of emotional vulnerability. However, Franco demonstrates that deep and meaningful friendships serve a unique purpose in our lives, releasing our spouse or partner from "the insurmountable expectation of being someone's everything" (8) and in some ways surpassing our romantic relationships in meeting certain needs. It is also clear that a good friendship is a critical aspect of the success of our relationship with a partner.

For our purposes in this book, when I talk about taking initiative to deepen a connection with a potential friend, I do not mean romantic partners. However, in the early stages of relationship development, the dynamics may feel similar. Perhaps this is why some men are uncomfortable with deeper emotional connection. Men are not often enculturated to connect to their own emotions and are uncomfortable with others' emotions. They often have the experience of sexualizing emotional connection. If a man feels an emotional connection, there is sometimes an assumption of physical or sexual attraction. For this reason, many heterosexual men are uncomfortable with deep emotional connections with other men. It is also why good friendships with women might feel easier but can be potentially problematic.

The fundamental difference between a good friendship and a romantic relationship is the lack of sexual intimacy in friendship. Friends might show affection in physical ways, but the expression of affection through a sexual relationship is generally reserved for romantic partners. At this point, someone might raise the question about the concept of "friends with benefits." Sexual energy is often expressed outside of a committed relationship, and sexual activity is often treated casually. However, the expression "making love" as a euphemism for sex grew out of the experience that having sex with someone is an intimate connection that enhances the bond between two people. In its ideal state, it is an expression of deep, committed love. While some people seem to navigate sexual relationships without romantic entanglements, as a psychotherapist, I have heard of innumerous occasions of sexual activity outside a committed relationship hurting at least one of the individuals. It can also be disastrous to relationships. While friendships can exist between heterosexual members of the opposite sex or between homosexual members of the same sex, it presents challenges that require another layer of communication and boundaries. (This is not the case when the friends are not in other committed relationships and the friendship has the potential to develop into more than a friendship.)

If partners in committed relationships develop friendships with others who may threaten the primary relationship, general guidelines might be helpful. Such relationships should always be known to the partner or spouse. The partner or spouse should not have concerns or reservations about the friendship. The friendship should be openly discussed, with nothing hidden about the nature of the relationship, the time spent together, or topics discussed. Such friendships can be problematic if they become secretive, are built around conversations about the primary relationship, or contain an element that neither of the friends would want to be widely known.

The focus of this book is the cultivation of friendships without a romantic threat to a primary romantic commitment and, generally, with appropriate boundaries. In general, I suggest that the deepening of friendships discussed in the remainder of this book is best expressed between friends without the possible complication of romantic attraction. My own experiences have been primarily, but not exclusively, with male friends. However, I believe that the qualities of good friendships have a more universal application and can enhance *any* relationship.

Developing Friendships

John E. Lyndon and others conducted research on developing friendships and found that as "Acquaintances" moved toward being "Friends," there was an increase in the significance assigned to certain behaviors and actions (Lydon 1997). They suggest a third category that emerged from their research: "transitional relationship" or "pre-friendship." These are relationships between acquaintances who wish to pursue a deeper friendship. In this type of relationship, interactions take on more meaning and there is greater scrutiny of the other's actions and reactions than before. When we seek to deepen our relationship with another person, we take more personal risks and make ourselves more vulnerable. This risk in connecting with another person requires courage and can sometimes feel like dating.

Many years ago, I realized that loneliness was a challenge for me, and I began to understand how I had contributed to keeping myself emotionally isolated. I decided to work on cultivating meaningful relationships with other men. I admired a few people at my workplace for certain qualities they seemed to have. I experienced others in social situations, like kids' school functions or church, and felt drawn to these people because of their personality or outlook. I began to invite certain men to have lunch with me. We met for a meal and a visit, and I asked about their lives and perhaps the qualities that I had observed, trying to learn how they had cultivated those qualities. I shared a few things about myself and tried to see if we had enough of a connection to meet again. That is when it felt like dating. Some lunches were pleasant, and I enjoyed the time, but did not feel a particular connection with the person. Other times, I appreciated the way a person talked about themselves; their seemingly genuine feelings; and their openness and honesty. I left those lunches thinking, "Man, I really like him. I wonder if he enjoyed our lunch as much as I did. I would like to visit with him again, but I don't know if I should suggest that or not." I have always had a bit of social anxiety, so I also questioned myself: "Maybe I shouldn't have said this or that. Maybe it was too much to ask about this thing or that. Maybe I was too much." Many times, I got a message or phone call from the person, saying, "Hey, I enjoyed lunch today. We should do that again. When could we do that?" I would feel like, "Yes! It wasn't just me!" That waiting and questioning of myself reflected my fear of being rejected. There is a risk in sharing yourself with another person. It is vulnerable and scary.

Most of my relationships that developed over lunches remained "lunch" relationships. Sometimes these friends and I attempted to get our wives or families together, but I think part of me liked having the time for some intimate sharing with another person who demonstrated that they could meet me at that place of connection. This began to affect the way I viewed the "dating" part of the lunches. I conceptualized the lunches as me exploring a deeper connection with another person. Not every person I went to lunch with wanted that or was capable of it, but some did and were. The connection began to feel less risky because I realized that if a person did not desire to meet again, there could be many reasons, but only some of those reasons might have something to do with me. Maybe they have enough friends. Maybe they are not looking for deeper connections with others. Maybe they have difficulty making time for such meetings. Or maybe they do not want to have the kinds of conversations I hope to have. Some are just not a good fit, but that does not mean they reject me.

Over the years, a few friends have met regularly with me for lunch or coffee to talk about our lives, our relationships, and ourselves. These chats are helpful to me because I feel I can be known by these people, and I can know them beyond the usual social interactions. I was not always comfortable sharing and could recognize my own fears about being vulnerable, but often, I would say so out loud. I once told my friend Kyle a story that reflected my own failings and struggles. He was quiet for a moment, and I said, "I'm curious what you're thinking. I'm afraid your silence means you're thinking badly about me now." His response was gracious. Even my confession of fear about his response opened the possibility of rejection, and our relationship may or may not have been able to bounce back. But Kyle's response was accepting and gracious, which made me feel safe. My vulnerability with others has often invited them to share at the same level of vulnerability with me, and the resulting conversations are meaningful and helpful.

Such conversations could occur over a meal, a game of golf, or a hot beverage at a kitchen table, but it is their substance and depth that make the relationship meaningful. In the coming chapters, we will continue to look at qualities and traits that help facilitate this level of connection.

Chapter 2

Therapeutic, Not Therapy

The key to successful psychotherapy is building a strong therapeutic relationship between therapist and client. Research has shown that the specific theoretical orientation of a therapist or the therapeutic techniques applied in psychotherapy are not as important for a positive outcome as the nature of the therapist-client relationship.[2] A relational focus is the source of connection and depth in psychotherapy but can also lead to sme misconceptions about how therapy and friendship are similar and different.

As I meet new clients or engage in general conversation, when people learn that I am a psychotherapist, I encounter a variety of comments that reflect common misconceptions. People often believe that therapy involves the therapist evaluating the client and telling them what to do. Many people start therapy a bit defensive (or avoid therapy altogether) because they are fearful of the therapist's judgement or correction. Other people have mocked the process of therapy by saying that therapists *never* tell you what to do and only "listen." Many people have asked me over the years, "Why should I pay you to listen to me when I could just be talking to a friend or family member?" The difficulty with these assessments is that they make incorrect assumptions about what therapy is and isn't. It is easy to see why some would be confused if they have never engaged in the process. People have experiences with "advisors" in their lives from whom they seek advice. Someone like a financial advisor will evaluate

---

2. See, for example, M. J. Lambert and D. E. Barley, "Research Summary on the Therapeutic Relationship and Psychotherapy Outcome," *Psychotherapy: Theory, Research, Practice, Training* 38/4 (2001): 357–61.

the person's situation and offer a plan for the person to improve money management or meet certain goals. A therapist might do some of this, but it is only a part of the process. There are also distortions of the therapeutic process portrayed in film and television that perpetuate misconceptions. Much of the psychotherapy on screen is used to develop a character or help advance the plot. The portrayal is either overly simplified or grossly distorted. Unfortunately, there are also people who practice some methods of "counseling" that contribute to these stereotypes. Many think that seeing a therapist is helpful simply because the therapist is supposed to be a neutral third party. It is true that an objective perspective is a critical part of psychotherapy, and it is true that friends and family are often biased in their responses and perspectives, but this alone is not what makes therapy unique.

What makes the process of psychotherapy different than talking with a friend or other type of helper is subtly complex. It involves the therapist's training, theoretical orientation, choice of supervisor of their clinical work, their own therapy, the setting and boundaries of the conversations, and the definition or intent of these conversations. The relationship between a client and a psychotherapist might feel *friendly*, but the relationship is not a friendship. While there may be some variation in what makes for a good therapeutic relationship, I wish to outline several qualities of a therapy relationship and highlight some that may translate into relationships between friends. Many of these elements require hundreds or thousands of hours of practice to cultivate, and no therapist ever gets the dynamics just right, but some of them might be adapted to help deepen relationships between friends.

In the beginning of his book, *Getting Started: An Introduction to Dynamic Psychotherapy*, Joel Kotin gives a simple definition of psychotherapy as "Two people talking together to be helpful to one of them," or as I sometimes paraphrase it, "A relationship between two people for the benefit of one of them." While this definition is simple, it captures an important difference between psychotherapy and friendship. In a therapy relationship, the focus should always be on the client, their needs, their growth, and their development.

Friendship is a relationship between two people for the benefit of *both* of them. This is not to say that therapists do not benefit from interacting with their clients, because they do, but the focus should always be on the client and the client's needs. Any benefit the therapist might experience is a byproduct and would rarely be discussed with a client. A conversation between friends may focus more on one of them at any given time, but the ideal is mutuality—give and take, sharing between both, support for both, and care for both. If a friendship feels like it is only benefiting one of the people in the relationship, it might be time to evaluate the friendship.

The Frame of Therapy

One of the basic elements of a therapeutic relationship is that it occurs within a particular set of guidelines and expectations. If you have ever been to see a psychotherapist, the therapist hopefully provided you some information about them and their practice that included expectations and guidelines about how often you might meet, the amount of time you will meet (length of a session), where you will meet, how much you will be charged for the session, guidelines for confidentiality, etc. A therapist might only provide service in a single location, or they might also provide services via video or by telephone or even at a client's home or office. The therapist should be clear about the guidelines and may have a separate set of guidelines if therapy is offered outside the traditional office setting. It would generally be considered problematic if a therapist said they only met clients in their office but agreed to meet a particular client at a coffee shop or at the client's home. Similarly, a therapist will always have a regular fee that they charge for a session of counseling. The length of that session will be defined, and the fee will be clear. Again, it is problematic if the therapist arbitrarily (or seemingly arbitrarily) changes their fee for certain clients. There should be clear guidelines for when an adjustment to a fee might be considered and under what circumstances that would happen. It is also generally considered problematic if a therapist regularly sees a particular client for more or less time than the stated length of a therapy session. These elements of time, location, and other guidelines are referred to as "the frame" of therapy. Bending or changing the frame of therapy should only be done with caution and intentionality.

Friendships do not have such formal frames, but there are often unspoken rules or social guidelines. Social rules of engagement might dictate which topics are talked about, how close we get to one another, or how much we share. For example, my "lunch friend" relationships involved conversations over a meal or a cup of coffee. It would have been a change of the unspoken frame to suggest meeting at a different time or location. You may have experienced this kind of dynamic when a friend came to your house for the first time. The person saw a part of your life they had not experienced before. They learned more about you than they may have known previously. You might have felt nervous about them coming. You probably cleaned the house well to present your home in the best way possible. The move from meeting at public places or knowing someone only in one place like school, church, work, etc. to inviting someone into your home involves a noticeable shift in the dynamic of the relationship. In friendships, such shifting of "the frame" occurs regularly, and friends generally do not ask each other, "How does it feel to see me in a new location?" When there is a shift of frame in therapy, it is the therapist's job to note the potential shift. "You usually see me in the evening," they might say. "What is it like for you to see me first thing on a Monday morning?" I currently see a client at seven in the morning (not my favorite time of day). Recently, we had to change our appointment because of a scheduling conflict. We agreed to meet at two in the afternoon. When the client walked in the door, she said, "It feels weird to see you in the afternoon and not first thing in the morning." A friend *could* ask about potential feelings regarding a change in time or location, but generally friends neither have the sensitivity to such feelings, nor are such feelings a regular part of social conversations.

Confidentiality

One of the most important parts of the therapy frame is confidentiality. A therapist's notes are considered medical or health records and are subject to laws governing the protection of such records.

There are also laws that require reporting of certain facts disclosed in therapy. Most therapists will provide their clients with a written copy of confidentiality policies, and they are required to provide a copy of their version of the federal requirements for the protection of medical records. However, a therapist may also verbally confirm these with a client before or at the beginning of the first session. I generally tell my clients, "Everything you say to me here will be kept here. I will not talk about you outside of here unless I have your written permission to do so. If you share with me that you are in danger of harming yourself or another person, or you give me information about the abuse of a child or a vulnerable adult, I am obligated by law to report that." Once we have this conversation, the client has my guarantee that this is the case. If at any point they learn that I have violated this policy, it not only becomes a breach of trust in the relationship but also a matter of legal and professional misconduct. I believe that once we have this conversation about confidentiality, if a client discloses reportable information to me, at some level they want this to be reported or they want some type of intervention. A therapist may handle reporting in various ways, but if such information is disclosed, the therapist should ensure that the information is reported appropriately.

Friends rarely make such agreements formally, but confidentiality facilitates trust and is a hallmark of meaningful relationships. As conversations deepen between friends and they become more vulnerable with one another, one or both might be aware of the risk they take in sharing something and ask, "Can we keep this between us?" The friends might agree to share only with certain others, like a spouse, but would not want some things shared beyond that. They make an informal agreement about rules of confidentiality. This is worth having an uncomfortable conversation rather than learning later that a friend shared something you believed was only between the two of you. One of the risks in clarifying the agreement is having someone ask for blanket confidentiality without knowing what they might disclose. Some things are not healthy to keep quiet, and some things may be illegal to keep. Several states in the United States have mandatory reporting laws for child abuse or other abuses. This means that *anyone* who becomes aware of abuse of a child must report it, or they can be held legally accountable for the abuse that occurs. It can also be dangerous to keep a secret about possible self-harm of your friend. Some areas may seem "gray" in this regard. If a friend is doing something that you do not like but is not fundamentally hurtful, it is challenging to know whether to intervene, especially when that might end the friendship. I suggest that if a person asks for blanket confidentiality before disclosing something, you offer a promise like, "I don't know what you are going to share, but I am happy to keep things between us unless you are in imminent danger or you tell me about the abuse of a child." That might sound awkward, but it is best to avoid promising to keep a friend's secret that you can't or shouldn't keep. Once you clarify your expectations about confidentiality, your friend can choose whether to go ahead and disclose what they wanted to share.

There is a difference between confidentiality and "secrets." People need the freedom to express their thoughts and feelings in a safe environment. In a therapy relationship, it is essential for the client to feel free to say what they want or need to say, in whatever way they want to say it. Sometimes the depth of feeling can lead people to say things that they keep inside most of the time and do not share with others in regular social settings. These feelings might come out in language that a person rarely uses otherwise. The use of profanity can reflect the depth of feelings. I will say more about listening and dealing with feelings later, but here I want to stress the importance of holding what a friend confesses without judgment and without reaction. If we overreact to what a person says or *how* a person says it, we decrease the possibility of them sharing with us again. Confidentiality allows another person to disclose something in trust, knowing that we will respectfully hold what is shared without judging or overreacting.

Secrets, on the other hand, are more destructive and insidious. When a person confesses that they have done something destructive or hurtful to themselves or another person, we cannot hold that in confidence for long. I had a professional friend with whom I visited regularly over lunch. During our conversation about our work one day, my friend disclosed to me some things he was doing in his practice that were at least unorthodox and potentially hurtful. I was not a supervisor to my friend, so I encouraged him to be careful and suggested he consult with a supervisor and talk to his own therapist about potential unmet personal needs that might be clouding his judgment. At the time, my friend had not crossed significant professional boundaries, but he was in a gray area. I had nothing concrete to report, but I was also not comfortable holding the information he gave me. I determined that my course of action was to encourage my friend to get the professional support that I believed would be beneficial for him.

Suppose a friend disclosed to you that they sometimes drink too much and hide this from their family, or they sometimes "lose it" with their kids, or they sometimes hurt themselves by cutting, or they binge on snack food or regularly starve themselves? What if a friend admitted a relationship with someone who is not their significant other? Each scenario might require additional information. You might want to know more of the details, but all of them are red flags that indicate potential problems. You could hold these secrets in confidence for a while, but you eventually should suggest that your friend get professional help. Abuse of a child is a reportable behavior. If your friend's alcohol use or eating disorder is not controlled, it can become dangerous, even life-threatening. We will consider dealing with difficult relationship issues in a later chapter, but remember there is a difference between "confidentiality" and "secrets." One helps build intimacy and deepens relationships, while the other can become dangerous or destructive.

Dual Relationships

For many people in our culture, asking for help does not come easily. Many people are comfortable offering help when it is needed but have difficulty being in need. It makes us vulnerable to possible judgment, to having things done in a way that is not helpful to us, and to disappointment or rejection. Asking someone to help us can reflect a shift in a friendship because it invites a deeper level of involvement in each other's lives. However, among friends, offering to do something for someone, to help them with a project, to babysit, to take food when someone is sick, and more are natural parts of friendship. Friends do favors for one another.

One complicated social convention is what we might call "score-keeping." For example, a person paid for my meal last time, so I need to pay for their meal this time. That couple invited us to their house, so we should invite them to our house. To a certain extent, mutuality is a reasonable expectation in relationships. However, it can also feel burdensome to keep up with the dynamic of whose turn it is. There are ways to navigate this without the anxiety of matching another person's gift. When someone does something for you, the only requirement is for you to say, "Thank you." There may be a time when you do something for someone who has done something for you, but the two events should not necessarily be tied to one another. It should not feel like an obligation. One of my "lunch friends" clarified at our first lunch, "I will buy my own lunch and you can buy yours." He said he did not like having to keep up with who paid last time or whose turn it was to pay. To make it clean and easy, he preferred that we pay for our own meals. In a manner of speaking, this became part of "the frame" of our meetings. We should do for others because we want to and not so we will get something back from them or because they did something for us. When we have unspoken expectations that are disappointed when the other person does not behave as we hoped, resentment may build. Luke 6:35 encourages us to "do good, and lend, expecting nothing in return." Doing good with the expectation of getting something in return is not true generosity. It results in resentment, which can kill relationships.

Some people consciously or unconsciously use the social expectation of matched favors to manipulate others into doing what they want. However, many people are not aware that they have this score-keeping mentality, but when others do not behave as they expect, they may think something like, "After all I have done for them!" We may not be aware that we are interacting at this level until the convention fails and our sense of expectation or even entitlement is exposed. We should give out of generosity, not obligation or an attempt to get what we want. Do not agree to do more than you are able or willing to do, and when others do for you, respond with gratitude. It is emotionally unhealthy when interactions are built on unspoken expectations of mutuality. While mutuality is a quality of good relationships, it must be freely given and freely expressed. If you find yourself thinking that you *have* to do for others or that they *should* do something for you, the relationship may need an adjustment.

One of the goals of psychotherapy is to avoid such issues by keeping expectations and the focus of the relationship clear. The objectivity of the therapist is essential. I noted earlier that objectivity is not *the* thing that makes therapy a unique relationship, but it is extremely important that the therapist seeks to avoid imposing his or her own will, views, insecurities, values, etc. on the client. To avoid this, the therapist needs to do their own therapy and regularly deal with their own issues. Therapists must also seek to avoid what is known as "dual relationships" with clients.

In most other professions, there is not a strong distinction between a client/customer and our friends. My father was a financial planner. Dad's clients and his friends were indistinguishable. He helped his friends with financial matters, and the people he met as clients regularly became friends. He never knew a stranger and struck up easy conversations with anyone anywhere. He moved fluidly between his personal life and his work life. There was no clear distinction between the two for him.

This is not true for therapists (or at least it should not be). Ideally, a therapist has only one purpose and role in the therapeutic relationship: to be the therapist to the client. The focus of therapy is on the client—what is best for the client and the client's situation. A therapist who feels lonely needs to deal with these feelings by seeing their own therapist or seeking out their own friends; they should not use their clients to meet social needs. Therapists do not date clients. Therapists do not have friends who are clients. And therapists do not act as a professional counselor to their friends.

This important piece of the therapeutic frame is often confusing. Clients usually feel a sense of connection with their therapists. (It is also true that therapists feel a sense of connection with their clients.) However, the connection exists within a particular context or frame.

Trying to extend the relationship beyond that frame damages the relationship and is often hurtful to the client. It is the therapist's job to monitor and hold the frame. Some clients have asked me about getting coffee or having lunch together. As much as I might enjoy that, the therapy relationship is not about me and my needs; it is about what is best for the client, and breaking the frame of therapy is rarely in the client's interest. It seems obvious to most people that a therapist would never engage in a romantic or sexual relationship with a client, but unfortunately many have, and it has destroyed trust and care in the relationship.

Challenges to therapeutic objectivity are not usually so blatant. Some of my clients have asked me for rides to or from my office. Even when that might be possible, it is a bend in the frame and may affect the therapy relationship. Some of my clients have offered to give me extravagant gifts, wanted me to buy Girl Scout cookies from their child, or asked me to come see them in a show at a local club. A therapist would ideally say no to all of these in the interest of focusing on the therapy relationship within the frame of therapy. However, when such things cannot be avoided, it is important to talk about the break. I have often had the opportunity to preach at a variety of churches. I have also led several professional workshops for therapists and others. At different times, a current client was present for one of these events. If we know ahead of time, we can talk about how we will handle such an event. If we do not know ahead of time, we will talk about it after the fact to process feelings and clarify any concerns. Years ago, one of my clients raised birds. My kids were interested in having a bird. It would have been easy to talk to my client about buying a bird from her, but she was my client, and my focus was being her therapist. What would have happened if the birds were unhealthy? What would have happened if one of the birds had died? What if I learned that the price I paid her was not a fair-market value? How would such things affect my relationship with the client and my objectivity?

Similarly, many of my friends who have endured various difficulties have asked to speak to me because I am a therapist. I have been clear that such people are my friends. We have a mutuality in our friendship. I get my emotional needs met in these relationships, and I help to meet theirs. I cannot be unbiased and do not want to give up the gift of friendship. One of my seminary professors of pastoral care said that in such situations, he asks his friends, "Which hat would you like me to wear as I listen—my therapist hat or my friend hat?" I appreciate the intent of this question, but it still implies a possible split in the relationship that does not exist. What I often say is, "I can't be your therapist, but I am your friend who is a therapist. I would be happy to visit and hear what's going on and offer resources that I might be aware of." In such a situation, I feel like I do listen differently than another person might. And I know of resources that others might not, but it is my job to support my friends and help refer them to appropriate resources for formal help. In subsequent conversations, I can ask how things are going. I can ask if the resources were helpful for them. I can offer care and support, but I am the friend, not the therapist.

Focusing on the relationship is important, and I have had significant conversations over the years around these issues. One client I saw was homeless for a time in her life. She often slept in her car and did not have enough to eat. When she came to my office, I sometimes had snacks in the waiting room that I could offer her. It was hard for me to resist giving her money, but I had to remember that my role was to be her therapist. During this time, I did agree to see her for free, and I worked for a counseling center that had resources to allow me to do this on a limited basis. Even so, the arrangement felt inadequate to me, and in one session I said to her, "It is so hard for me to see you in this situation, and I feel like what I have to offer you is so insignificant when you don't have enough to eat or a place to stay." With tears in her eyes she said, "You will never know how much it means to me to be able to come here and talk with you. I have no other place in my life where I can talk about these things."

Similarly, I saw another client years ago who had suffered significant abuse. She was obviously uneasy in several of our first sessions. In one of the sessions, I asked her about her concerns or fears, and she said, "I keep waiting for the day that I come in here and you ask me to take off all of my clothes." I was able to say with confidence that this would never happen and that my office would be a safe place for her. It was essential that therapy be a safe place for her and that her experience with me as a male therapist was dramatically different from her relationships with other men in her life. The frame of therapy is important and creates safety. The frame of friendship is usually less formal, but the boundaries can be equally important.

Summary

While therapy can feel friendly, the relationship between therapist and client is not a friendship but a professional relationship designed to assist the client. I would suggest that a good friendship can be quite therapeutic, but it is not therapy. A therapy relationship has a number of structures and expectations to protect the therapist's objectivity and the client's safety. This is achieved through clear communication and expectations by a trained therapist. Friendship often has structures and expectations that are not formal or overt, and they are generally not rigid. Friendship is a mutual relationship that benefits both friends. Some of the elements that make a therapy relationship meaningful for a client in psychotherapy are skills that friends could adapt to enhance their relationship. We will look further at these in the following chapters.

Chapter 3

Listening & Sharing for Deeper Connection

One of the most common complaints of couples in therapy is difficulty with communication. This is often caused by some common breakdowns in communicating with each other. Partners may think they are saying what they intend to say, but they are not as clear as they believe. Partners may have experiences, insecurities, biases, and more that cause them to add meaning and interpretation to their partner's words so that they hear something unintended. The partners may try to avoid direct communication or direct conflict and therefore communicate in incomplete, indirect, and vague ways. Finally, sometimes partners are communicating well, but one or both of them are fixed in their expectations or desires, and they do not like or refuse to accept what the other is saying. To some extent, these pitfalls can affect any relationship. However, in less intimate relationships, communication difficulties are more likely to be dealt with by dismissing, avoiding, or cutting off the other person. We will look at dealing with conflicts in chapter 6, but in this chapter I will discuss cultivating communication skills that can help avoid breakdowns in connection before they become a problem. The first step toward good communication is learning how to listen. Listening well begins by knowing what to listen for, how to clarify what is heard, and how to respond.

Humble Curiosity

I recently led a Bible study on Matthew 18 and 19, where Jesus has the opportunity to interact with children. My reflections from the lesson centered on two questions: "What are the qualities of childlikeness that we need to cultivate in order enter the kingdom of heaven?" (Matt 18:3-4), and "What are the qualities of life that make us more welcoming of children in our lives?" (19:13-15). Two major ideas emerged from these questions. Children have great curiosity about the world around them. Young children do not judge what they observe; they must be taught to do that. Unfortunately, by the time they are older, they may have learned to ostracize, tease, and bully those with differences, but younger children just have a sense of curiosity. They explore the world with all their senses. They do not judge people and will smile and be friendly to a perfect stranger. Related to this curiosity is their sense of awe and wonder. Adults can become desensitized and jaded. We might lose that childlike sense of wonder about the world. As we get older, we learn what it is to be hurt, and we become more careful about our connections. We grow self-conscious and afraid of others' judgment, so we don't dance with vigor, we don't do things that make us feel silly or inept, and we look with suspicion on those who do. To change and become like a child, as Jesus says, involves a mindfulness and intentionality to slow down and appreciate the beauty of the world around us. It means letting go of others' expectations and judgments and living a life that feels right for us and is not dictated by what others might think. It also means we seek to rid ourselves of tribal mentalities that divide the world into "us" and "them" in order to protect our place and our group.

Another major idea from that recent Bible study is related but somewhat different. I thought of how easy it is for us to have a sense of self-importance. Our lives, our agendas, our jobs, and our commitments all seem very important. The child who wants to show us a flower they have just discovered or wants to ask about something they have seen might seem like a trivial distraction. The disciples tried to send the children away, saying that Jesus was too important for them, but Jesus said, "Let them come; don't stop them." In order for us to make room for children, we have to maintain perspective about our work and our lives. We have to cultivate a mindfulness that includes time for things that could feel trivial. Most of all, we must cultivate a sense of humility. We should not be too big or too important to make time for children. As I write, I am thinking of clients I have seen who would read these words and immediately feel guilty because they were impatient with their children yesterday. That is not my intent. Every adult has been impatient with a child (or someone) at times. My goal is not to condemn that but to note the broad attitudes of the heart that allow us to take time for children regularly and to recognize their play and their feelings as significant.

These attitudes of humility, curiosity, and wonder are keys to being a good listener and a caring presence. We must be able to set aside our sense of self-importance, our personal agendas, and our initial perceptions. This is essential for a good therapist, and it is essential for good conversations anywhere. When we talk with someone and they share something we do not like or do not understand, we should try not to respond from the place of a jaded, judgmental adult and say, "Why did you do that?" or "That is not right" or, worse, "That's stupid." We can acknowledge that we might see something differently, but with humility we should respond out of curiosity. We might say something like, "I have never thought of things like that" or "I'm not sure I understand what you mean" and then add, "Tell me more about that." Any question that invites more information is helpful, but a judgment or correction will probably end the conversation.

One of my pet peeves is the provocative email that comes to my inbox regularly. These have subjects like "You're drinking wine all wrong," "You're cooking your steak all wrong," or "You're [fill in the blank] all wrong." I hate these emails for a number of reasons, but the biggest is because they presume a proper way to do everything and create an opportunity for us to feel inadequate or stupid. Such messages also feed into our fears of appearing inept or unsophisticated to others and encourage us to judge one another by how we do something. These types of emails (and attitudes) raise our anxiety about being correct or proper, presupposing that there is only one way to be human. I would suggest that in most things, there is more than one way to do something, whether decorating a house, wearing clothing, playing music, drinking wine, cutting the grass, or anything else. Each of us has our preferred way to do something while someone else may have a different way. Objectively, there may be a way to do something that leads to be better outcome in one way or another. However, if I want to share that with another person, I would not say, "The right way is . . . ." Instead, I might say, "I have found that when I do it this way . . . ." This approach leaves the other person with the autonomy to make their own decisions about the way they do things. There are, of course, some limits. This way of thinking may not apply when the safety or well-being of another person is at risk or if a technical procedure is involved. I would not want my surgeon to decide to operate "his way" when the time comes to make an incision. However, many innovations occur when someone decides to challenge conventional wisdom and risk trying something innovative. When it comes to a desire for better relationships and conversations, we can share our way, but things will go much better if we set aside our preconceived ideas and engage the other person with curiosity.

I don't think of myself as a huge coffee drinker. When I drink coffee, I don't just go into any random place and pour a cup of whatever coffee they have, even if they provide creamer and sugar. I do not drink plain black coffee anywhere. I am a froufrou coffee drinker, or as I often say, "I like coffee-flavored beverages." I generally drink lattes or mochas. If I were sitting with someone who said, "Once you put all that stuff in your coffee, you're not really drinking coffee the proper way. According to this or that authority, coffee ought to be consumed this way or that way," I would not feel safe. I would feel shamed for how I drink coffee and less likely to want to spend time with my pretentious friend or open up to them about anything. (At this point in my life, I would not necessarily be intimidated by this and might push back, but my younger self would have shut down.) However, if I was with someone who asked, "Do you always drink lattes or do you drink coffee different ways?" I would respond with my spiel about not being a coffee drinker (despite my habit of having two or three cups a day) and how I drink coffee-flavored beverages. They might reply that they love coffee and feel they can taste it better if there is nothing in it, but it is presented as their preference and not necessarily as a comment on my froufrou coffee. Someone's preference should not feel like an attack on me or my preference but an exchange between two autonomous peers.

The same kind of dynamics can exist about more difficult subjects like beliefs, religious practices, political ideas, etc. Humble curiosity is a great place to begin. When the other person shares their story or their view, look for what you can affirm. Search for something in common. "Oh, I see how that would be meaningful," or "I see why that would be important." Maybe ask for more information, or ask for clarification. In friendships and other relationships, you might share how you experience things or how you view things differently, but share from a place of humility and respect for the other person with a goal of maintaining the relationship. If you encounter someone who is open and curious and willing to engage in mutual curiosity, the conversation can be incredibly rewarding. The reality is that not every person with whom we might engage is able to reciprocate. Not everyone is open to similar exchanges. That is ok. Even if we know we can't connect with a person at that level, we can keep our hearts of humble curiosity regardless.

Listen to Understand, Not to Fix

When we honestly ask ourselves which person in our lives means the most to us, we often find that it is those who, instead of giving advice, solutions, or cures, have chosen rather to share our pain and touch our wounds with a warm and tender hand. The friend who can be silent with us in a moment of despair or confusion, who can stay with us in an hour of grief and bereavement, who can tolerate not knowing, not curing, not healing and face with us the reality of our powerlessness, that is a friend who cares. (Henri Nouwen, *Out of Solitude: Three Meditations on the Christian Life*, 2004)

I first read this quote several years ago and was struck by the profound truth reflected in Henri Nouwen's words. Over the years, several good therapists and friends have embodied this for me. Many of us have had a personal experience with such friends, but when we listen to someone share struggles or hurts, we might feel the need to offer something to help or fix the situation. In trying to find that magic response, we might say things that have the opposite effect and hurt or alienate the other person. As a therapist and former hospital chaplain, I still can fall into the temptation of trying to fix a situation by offering advice or solutions. There are times when this might be appropriate, but the most important thing we can do is be present, offer empathy, and communicate that the other person is seen and understood. There is something profoundly healing in that.

A few months ago, as I was dealing with a particular issue in my life, I was in a session with my own therapist talking about the various things I felt. My therapist asked good, clarifying questions and often simply repeated back or paraphrased what I had said. As I talked, I was able to gain clarity about my thoughts and feelings and to develop an idea of how to deal with the situation. This situation did not have a clear fix and the shift I needed was in how I was thinking about it. As we came to the end of the session, I observed, "You know I have been doing this kind of work (both as the therapist and the client) for over twenty-five years, and I am still amazed at how therapy can feel like some kind of 'hocus pocus magic'— how just talking things through can be helpful. I feel so much better about this situation now than when I first sat down today." However, it is not "hocus pocus" but actual science that being heard and feeling understood are, indeed, powerful medicine.

This is definitely one of the aspects of therapy that is possible within a good friendship. For all of us, life can bring a variety of challenges—conflicts, changes, tragedies, losses. Many, if not all, people have the ability to process these events and return to a previous state of functioning. But sometimes the magnitude of challenges or challenges that come too quickly in succession can feel like getting knocked down by a wave at the beach and then being hit by another one before we can get our feet under us and stand up. We don't necessarily need someone to fix the problem; we just need someone to give us support while we get our feet back under us, and then we can move forward. The ability to be present and helpful without having "to fix" things is a skill to cultivate and hone. Many factors contribute to being present in this way, and there are many reasons why it is difficult for us. The abilities to listen well, to be a non-anxious presence, and to know what to focus on in a conversation are important tools for a therapist and a good friend. The following skills can enhance the connection in your own relationships.

Active Listening

To truly hear what someone says, you must listen to understand rather than listening to fix or change the other person. Trust is built when people feel heard and understood. If people feel you are judging their situation or trying to fix them or their problem, they will not feel like they can trust you and share with you. Practice the art of "humble curiosity," realizing that when a person shares with you, only about 7 percent of what they say is communicated by their words. Thirty-eight percent is communicated by their tone of voice, and 55 percent is communicated by their body language. The combination of words, tone, and body language has been called the "encoding" of the message (Savage 1996, 16). Decoding the message involves paying attention to words, tone, and body language, but it is complicated by what you bring to the conversation as the "receiver" of the message. Your fears, anxiety, life experiences, and beliefs will influence how you interpret the message and affect how you "decode" it. Being a good listener involves making sure you understand the received message without adding your own distortions.

Because being able to discern your feelings, reactions, and potential distortions is such an important part of listening and being present for others, going through a process of psychotherapy with the purpose of growth and self-understanding can be helpful. Processing our own hurts and working through our own struggles means that when others share, we are less likely to project our experiences into their stories. We are less likely to allow our deficiencies and insecurities to drive our interpretations and responses. We are also less likely to jump to conclusions about what a person means or what we think they feel. As you continue through this book, I hope to reveal ways that a good friend can assist in our self-awareness and self-discovery, but there is no true substitute for a course of good psychotherapy oriented toward insight and self-discovery. Such awareness gives us the ability to recognize feelings but not be driven by them. We are more capable of following the encouragement to "Be angry but do not sin" (Eph 4:26). We can allow ourselves to feel feelings and choose how to express them rather than acting out of feelings we do not yet understand. Going through therapy is not the *only* way to be a good listener, however. We can get better by practicing skills that at first may feel awkward.

One of the easiest ways to verify whether we are receiving the appropriate message from someone in a conversation is to repeat what we hear. If a person shares a longer narrative, we might offer a paraphrase of it. If a friend describes recent difficulty sleeping, lack of energy, and lack of appetite and then says, "I think I might be a little depressed since my dad died last year," you might say, "So since last year when your dad died, you have been having difficulty sleeping, feeling a lack of energy and loss of appetite, and you feel like you might be depressed." It may seem awkward to repeat the person's words back to them, but it signals that you have listened and heard what they said. I am still amazed that in therapy, this simple tool can elicit a surprised response from a client: "Yes! You really understand me." Saying or paraphrasing what a person said can help them feel heard and understood because you are indeed listening well enough to pay attention to them. When I was in training, one of my supervisors regularly said that our clients are our best supervisors. If we say something wrong or paraphrase something incorrectly, the other person will often correct us. For example, if in the above scenario I reply, "So since last year when your dad died, you have been experiencing sleeplessness, lack of energy, and loss of appetite *because you miss your dad*," the other person might respond, "I don't know if it's that I *miss* him as much as I have just felt depressed. I'm not sure why right now." The addition of "miss" in our paraphrase reflects our interpretation of what was shared, and the friend will realize that we have not truly heard the intended message. Most "mistakes" in interpretation are minor, but others can be problematic in a relationship. We will talk more about this in chapter 6.

Another way to engage someone about what they are sharing is to ask questions. This is a trickier because what we ask is important and depends on a number of factors. The biggest is perhaps the nature of your relationship with someone. Does a trusting foundation exist, or have you at least agreed that you seek to establish such a relationship with this person? A deep question might feel scary or threatening to someone with whom we have no foundation of trust and might push them away rather than inviting them to share more. In general, when asking a question feels appropriate, try to make it open-ended. Questions that elicit a single answer or a "yes" or "no" do not generally bring about a deeper understanding and often reflect a particular interpretation or bias on our part. There are times when we might ask such questions, but in general we should ask them sparingly and with humility. Similarly, the question "Why?" is generally a bad question. Asking why, even in a non-threatening manner or about a seemingly benign matter, can cause defensiveness as the other person tries to explain the decision or action. Continuing the example from above of the depressed friend, I would not want to follow up with a question like, "Don't you miss your father?" or "Do you think your depression is a form of grief?" (The depression might be a form of grief, but a yes-or-no question implies an attempt fix it by defining the problem for the person and eliminating any nuance.) A better question might be, "How did you feel about your father?" or "What was your relationship with your father like?" These open-ended questions invite more information by encouraging your friend to share more of themselves.

Be aware that if you've had a long and comfortable relationship with a friend, you can ask such questions easily. If you do not know the person well, you might ask permission to ask such a question or give the person permission not to answer. For example, "I don't know if it is something you want to share with me, but what was your relationship with your father like?" or "I realize this might be too personal, so don't feel like you have to answer, but . . . ." This gives the person permission to share or go deeper if they want but also allows them to refrain. Even recognizing that your question might feel invasive communicates that you are a sensitive and safe listener.

Another simple question is more implied: an invitation to continue. You might ask, "Can you tell me more about that?" This question invites the other person to keep sharing and offer greater detail. As a person shares, you might notice that they skip certain pieces of information or a section of time. With humility and sensitivity and in an appropriately close relationship, you might say, "I noticed that you skipped a bit of your story. Would you like to tell me about that?" Noting missing or deleted information and being curious can feel intrusive. The person consciously or unconsciously skipped information either because they deemed it unimportant or because it would be uncomfortable to share. If you truly seek to be a helpful friend, avoid questions that are primarily motivated by your own curiosity. Or acknowledge your curiosity, but always leave the other person with the freedom to respond or not.

A less threatening approach can still be helpful. In my training, I was taught to "follow the feelings" and "follow affect." It is cliché that therapists ask, "How did that make you feel?" or "How did you feel when that happened?" The wording of these questions is significant. We do not control our feelings; we can control how we express them. When things happen, we have feelings about them. Things don't "*make* us feel." We feel when things happen. Identifying and understanding our feelings and reactions to various events can give us power and freedom to choose what we do next. So, while it is a cliché, it is important to ask how a person felt in a given situation. Some people have no idea how they felt. Others might be ashamed of how they felt, and still others might be able to tell you about it. "What were you feeling when this happened?" or "How did you feel when . . . ?" are important questions. Your comfort with certain feelings might affect how you react or respond to your friend's disclosure, so be prepared to manage your responses and feelings in the moment. For example, in the example about the friend who feels depressed, if I ask about feelings, my friend may confide, "I feel a little ashamed, but one of the biggest feelings I have had is relief." (Note that relief is a common feeling in many grief situations, but people who experience it sometimes feel guilty or ashamed because they believe they should feel more sadness.) Further conversation might reveal why your friend feels ashamed to say this and why they are relieved. You may even learn that part of their depression results from not feeling like they can share their relief.

As noted previously, people communicate volumes by something other than their words. Noting a person's facial expression, tone of voice, and body language can give us big clues about their feelings. In normal, everyday conversations with acquaintances and casual friends, we might notice these things, but we usually do not talk about them. But we can be more attentive in a relationship with a foundation of trust and a common goal of openness and honesty. Telling someone that when they talked about a particular subject their voice got louder or softer, that they physically drew themselves up in their chair and hugged their legs, or that they reacted some other way can lead to deeper, more revealing conversations. Try not to assume that you know why a person reacts a certain way or expresses a certain emotion. Set your ideas and agendas aside and approach your friend with openness and curiosity. A friend may begin to cry when telling you about a recent experience. You might think you know why they are crying, but it can be helpful to ask about it: "While you were talking, I saw your tears. What are you feeling?" Some listeners get uncomfortable when strong feelings, especially anger or sadness, are expressed. Part of maintaining a non-anxious presence is learning to manage our reactions to a person's feelings, not rushing in to fix things, and allowing them to go through the experience. When a friend cries about a situation, many people either try to give comfort with words of encouragement or feel overwhelmed by the emotion and advise the friend that they should not feel that way. Some listeners may even leave! The friend may interpret that they are "too much" or a burden. Attempting to alleviate a friend's emotion is usually more about helping us feel more comfortable than helping the friend (see more on this below).

In the same way that we should not assume what another person is feeling, when they talk about events or beliefs or use certain labels or terms, we should not assume we know what those terms mean. What I mean by having faith in God might be different than what someone else means. The same can be true if I refer to someone as "religious" or "lazy." How I think about those terms may not be what another person means by them. Clarification is helpful. If a friend says, "I was so upset that I fell apart at work," I might be curious what "upset" means in that context because it has a variety of connotations. I might also be curious what "fell apart" means. My idea of "falling apart" may not be what it is for other people.

If we have the goal of being better listeners, want to maintain a nonjudgmental and non-anxious presence, and believe that friendship is mutual, where do our own thoughts and feelings come in? In conversation with another person, we may hear them make a point or talk about something we have experience with and immediately want to share our own thoughts or experiences. Sometimes that is helpful, and sometimes the other person may feel that we have dismissed what they shared as unimportant. We must listen attentively as described above before we share our own experiences. We should be sure to share something about ourselves that relates to the person's actual situation, and we can only do that if we fully understand their experience. The other person should be confident that they are heard and understood.

Just as the majority of what the other person communicates is nonverbal, you as the listener also communicate a great deal nonverbally. If your friend is talking and you are looking at your phone or watching other people, the friend will not know for sure if you are listening or paying attention. We begin sharing ourselves by demonstrating interest in the other person. As a person talks, I might think I know what they are talking about, but I need to listen to all that they say rather than making assumptions about what I think they will say. When we decide to share about ourselves, we should ask ourselves why we are sharing. Maybe a friend shares about a wonderful beach experience, and we respond that we have also had a wonderful beach experience at the same place or a different place. This is a point of connection. However, a friend might share about a personal struggle or something that evokes strong emotion. If you intend to demonstrate that you connect with the experience, be sure that what you share will affirm the other person's situation and normalize what they are going through.

We will talk about responding to a person in crisis in a later chapter, but for now I urge us not to miss the other person's intent or trivialize what they share by comparing a personal experience that is not parallel to theirs. Imagine that your friend is in the hospital with a major, life-threatening infection and you say, "I understand. I had the flu a couple of months ago, and I felt terrible." Or your friend talks about a devastating breakup with a significant other and you respond, "Oh, I know how that is. I had two people break up with me in high school." In these examples, the responses are not in line with the original sharing. The person who shared will probably not feel heard or understood. If you have not had an experience that can truly help you identify with the person, either do not share it or share it with a caveat. "You know, I've been sick before and felt bad, but I can't imagine what that was like for you." "I've never had a breakup with someone that significant before. I can't imagine how you're feeling."

A Non-anxious Presence

As mentioned earlier, the idea of being a non-anxious presence is an important concept in pastoral care and counseling. The concept is part of Carl Rogers's person-centered therapy and also applies in Murray Bowen's family systems theory. The two methods are somewhat different, but both can apply in good conversations and meaningful friendships. First, being a non-anxious presence means being able to listen to another person and experience their displays of emotion without demonstrating strong emotional reaction, judgment, or disgust. It involves maintaining the posture of curiosity and humility about what they share and accepting their words without impulsive reaction. The concept is applied like this in person-centered therapy.

The second application, from family systems theory, is built on the observation that anxiety is contagious. When another person is upset, anxious, or frustrated about something, it can be easy for others to become anxious about it too. This anxiety often manifests in a need to fix the problem. This might look like an attempt to calm a friend or relieve their feelings because we are uncomfortable.

It might also involve moving into problem-solving to try to help someone accomplish a stated goal, either by giving advice or seeking to do something to try to make the situation better.

In systems theory, the idea of contagious anxiety is sometimes expressed in terms of "intergenerational transfer of anxiety"; the members of one generation become anxious about something and then try to control, manipulate, or avoid such issues for subsequent generations, passing their anxiety to their children and grandchildren. A classic example is a person who grew up in a household with an alcoholic parent. That person has observed and experienced the adverse effects, pain, and shame of living in such a family and consciously or unconsciously vows that they will not bring this into their own home when they are grown. For this reason, the person avoids drinking alcohol and may insist that their spouse, children, and others never touch alcohol either. The subject becomes taboo. Such anxiety can play out around any number of issues: money, vocation, pets, religion, sex, or place of residence.

Early in my training I met with a person who was preparing for a profession that required a professional degree. This person was seeing me because of a few setbacks in the process, and it was perceived that they were sabotaging their own success. After a good conversation about the person's early life, I learned that they had come from a working-class family and were the only person from their family to attend college, let alone pursue a professional degree. The family had ridiculed this person, referred to them as "uppity," and accused them of thinking they were better than the rest of the family. This seemed to reflect more of the family's anxiety and insecurity, but it left my client anxious, feeling torn between the dreams of becoming what they were preparing for and maintaining good standing with the family.

Similarly, I met a woman once who was interested in learning the violin when she was a child. However, her mother had forbidden her to take violin lessons because the mother's own mother had forced her to take lessons and it had been very unpleasant for her. The mother had never considered that she could manage the lessons with less intensity and allow her daughter to have her own experience of playing the violin rather than forbidding lessons altogether.

These examples point to the importance of being able separate our personal experiences from those of someone else and allowing that person to have their own experience and feel their own feelings. We can do this by remaining calm (non-anxious), staying curious, and exploring the other's experience rather than assuming a particular feeling or experience.

In psychotherapy, the therapist generally keeps their own experience to themselves and does not share with the client unless there is a good reason to do so and the therapist believes it would help the client. In a relationship between friends, the separation of one's own experience and their friend's experience is important, but friends can enjoy a good exchange about their experiences. It is normal for one friend to share an experience of a related event (assuming that they are related and equivalent, as noted earlier).

Transference & Countertransference

Psychologist George Kelly had a theory of experience called "Construct Theory." In his theory, each experience a person has creates a construct by which they evaluate and sort future experiences. I have conceptualized this with music. I have a large music collection and like a variety of types of music. When I hear a new song or artist, I immediately start comparing the sound what I have heard before. "This sounds like George Jones" or "This has a classic soul sound like the Temptations." There are times when an artist or genre is so unique that I need a new category or construct for it, but previous experience is the beginning of my evaluation. Similarly, if we grew up in an abusive home or were betrayed by a significant other, this can shape the way we experience subsequent events and may cause us to assume that the new event is just like the historic event. Any time there is a gap in the available information, we will make up things to fill in the missing pieces. We rarely fill those gaps with our best selves. If we were hurt or betrayed in the past, then when a person close to us does something we do not understand, we might automatically assume the worst of their intentions because of the "construct" of our previous experience. When this happens in psychotherapy, it is called "transference." Transference is the client's experience of something the therapist says or does. It can be positive or negative.

Years ago, I had the opportunity to be the "patient" in a process of psychoanalysis. This was a form of intense psychotherapy, like the stereotype one might see in a movie or television show where the patient lies on a couch with the analyst sitting at the head of the couch. The patient reflects on experiences, dreams, thoughts, feelings, etc. and essentially talks to the ceiling as the analyst takes notes and asks poignant questions to help uncover unconscious (or semiconscious) thoughts, feelings, or motivations. Traditional psychoanalysis usually occurs several times a week and often for many years. I was lucky enough to work with an analyst in training and was able to see her for a reduced fee while I was still in training as a therapist myself. I went four days a week for three years. This was probably the best process of self-discovery I have ever had, resulting in what I refer to as a "complete rewiring of my brain." It was truly transformational. During my time in analysis, my analyst would take regular vacations or be gone for a variety of reasons. Each time she planned to be away, she would start asking me to share any feelings I might have about her being gone at least two weeks before she left. In the beginning, I would always say something like, "No. I don't have any feelings about your being gone. I will miss seeing you, but I am glad you have the time away."

After we had been meeting for over a year, my analyst began asking me to share how I felt about an upcoming absence she had planned. For some reason, that time I began to cry. Then I judged the fact that I was crying. "This is so stupid!" I said. "You are only going on vacation. Why am I crying?!" My analyst began to explore my feelings and ask questions to guide my reflections. I noticed a deep sadness at the thought of her being gone, and I also felt a sense of betrayal or abandonment because she was leaving me. As we talked, we realized that this experience fit with what I might now call a "construct" from my childhood. The feeling of being left or betrayed had nothing to do with my analyst and everything to do with me. This is transference.

It is also true that a therapist can have similar experiences with their clients. This is why it is vitally important that a therapist does his or her own therapy to minimize being blindsided by personal feelings. When a therapist's issues are brought up because of the client sitting in front of them, it is called "countertransference." The objectivity that is so helpful to a client can be sabotaged if the therapist is unable to sort out his or her own experiences from those of the client. When I was in training, I met with a couple in which one of partners was dealing with a terminal diagnosis. Though I had worked as a hospital chaplain and interacted with dying clients, something about this couple's situation had me stuck. I brought the details of a particular session to my supervisor, and we reviewed a recording of my work with the couple. My supervisor observed the types of questions I was asking and noted my seeming discomfort in the session. My supervisor astutely asked me about my feelings regarding my own mortality. As I reflected on this, again I began to cry. Like my time in psychoanalysis, my tears were confusing to me, but I was able to talk about this with my supervisor and later talk to my analyst. Together, we worked out some feelings about loss and my own mortality. The clients' issues brought up my own issues. I was not able to separate my feelings from theirs until I got the supervision and therapy I needed to sort things out.

Transference and countertransference occur in many of our relationships. We might have difficulty with a boss because he reminds us of our father. We might have a friend who struggles with something that reminds us of a significant event in our own life, and it is hard to sort out our feelings. Often, such feelings and clouding of perception occur just outside of our conscious awareness. If we understand that all of our feelings and reactions may not be what they seem at first, we might gain enough humility about ourselves and our experiences to discover something new. We will talk more about how we react and defend ourselves in the next chapter.

Content vs. Process

When we become aware of the complexity of our feelings and our interactions with others, we recognize an internal dialogue that affects our actions, reactions, and experiences at any given time. In any conversation, there are things that we talk about and there is also our internal dialogue and feelings about what we say aloud. Many of those internal experiences might be connected to transference or countertransference. In the therapeutic process, we think about these two layers of conversation as "content" and "process." Content is whatever you are talking about, and process is the experience or feeling of talking about it. More meaningful conversations often occur when we move from the content of a conversation to explore the process. That is, we move from talking about something to *talking about talking about it.* A person might share with us something they have rarely shared with another person. We might say to them, "Thank you for trusting me with this information. How did it feel to share that with me?" What a person shared is the *content.* How the person felt about sharing is a *process* question. Imagine a friend says they want to share something with you, but they are afraid. Asking the person what they fear might happen if they share is a process question that may help the sharing feel safer.

Another type of process question involves exploring what a body posture, facial expression, or gesture means. We might note that when we talked about a particular subject or person, our friend made a certain face or reacted in a certain way. We might observe, "I noticed when we talked about that issue, you seemed to have a reaction to it. Do you want to talk about that?" The internal experience of the other person is more process oriented. Similarly, noting our own internal experience and drawing on it for conversation is significant. We might note to a friend, "I notice that as you're talking about this, I feel anxious. I'm not sure what that's about, but I wonder if you're also feeling that or if it's something about me that I need to look at." The friend might respond with an opportunity to tell them more or to reflect on what is happening. Or, in another situation, a friend might ask if we have someone we can talk to who can help us unpack such strong feelings. This awareness of our feelings can also benefit the other person. As another person shares their experience, we might say, "I feel so sad when you talk about this." The other person may or may not experience what they are sharing as sad, and your feelings may help them identify their own feelings.

A client of mine recently described a disagreement with his significant other. My client asked a question of the partner and got a bigger, more emotional response than anticipated. My client thought his question was more innocuous. He described how he later talked with his partner about the reaction. He said something like, "I'm confused by your reaction to my question earlier. Can we talk about what prompted such a strong response?" He described how the partner engaged in the conversation, and they resolved the issue and came to a better understanding that should help with future inter-actions. Moving that conversation from the content of the question to the process of what it felt like to the partner allowed for a better conversation about what the partner was thinking and feeling.

Summary

As many of us learned during the Covid-19 pandemic, we can communicate by video or phone, but the experience is not the same as sitting with someone in person. Our words are only a small part of how we communicate. Our body language, facial expressions, and intonation all play a part in encoding a message. As we listen to one another, part of listening is paying attention to try to decode the message. Many factors can interfere with our ability to communi-cate or decode a message. In order to be a better listener, we need to be aware of our own feelings and reactions and seek to be open to receiving whatever is communicated. We should try to respond from a non-anxious presence and remain curious about ourselves and the other person. The way we respond to someone, the questions we ask, and our facial expressions and reactions play a big part in whether others experience us as a safe person to talk to.

Chapter 4

Common Defenses that Inhibit Connection

Deepening relationships require vulnerability, and vulnerability always involves risk. We do not always know if our relationship with someone is safe and mutual. Working to construct such a relationship takes time and intentionality. Whether we feel safe is not just dependent on the reactions of the other person but is also influenced by our previous experiences and our "constructs." As I noted in chapter 1, when Adam and Eve realized that they were naked (vulnerable), they immediately covered themselves. There was no reason to believe the other person intended harm because they had no previous experience of harm. Their desire to hide themselves seems to imply an internal experience of being seen and fearing judgment. They looked around and the first coverings they saw were fig leaves. It is interesting that when Adam and Eve finally encountered God and confessed what had happened, God did not undo the consequence of their actions. Adam and Eve were not returned to a state of innocent nakedness; God simply made them better coverings. Sometimes we cannot undo the consequences of our actions, and in our own shame we create ways to cover and protect ourselves. In chapter 1 we looked at the development of our "shadow side" made of aspects of ourselves and our experiences that we attempt to hide and/or disown. We use various defenses to keep others from seeing our shadow sides. These strategies can also protect *us* from seeing our shadow sides.

Our defenses are usually unconscious or semiconscious reactions that are more automatic than intentional. Like the fig leaves of Adam and Eve, they hide parts of us, but they are only effective to a point. Remember that Adam and Eve immediately began to blame others for their disobedience (Gen 3). Adam blamed Eve and Eve blamed the serpent. Blaming others for our bad behavior or mistakes is an example of a defense strategy. We blame other people to maintain an inward image that we are blameless. If someone else's influence caused us to do something, then we might perceive that we are still good or perfect. However, if we become aware of what we are hiding and why, and if we explore our feelings and allow ourselves to deal with what we find, then we can grow into a more complete self with the potential for deeper connections. This can occur in a healthy relationship with good communication, but it requires awareness and intentionality.

Of course, having the courage to be vulnerable to deeper connection does not mean walking around naked, literally or figuratively. People who share their pain indiscriminately are not being vulnerable. Sharing in this way is generally off-putting because it violates our socially accepted pattern of deepening relationships and is usually too much, too soon, occurring without a foundation of trust and mutuality. This manner of sharing (being emotionally naked all the time) fails to build connection and usually results in disappointment or rejection. Having the courage to be vulnerable is not walking around naked; it is instead choosing (hopefully wisely) the people with whom we wish to be *that* vulnerable. Disclosure is generally progressive, and each revelation with a positive outcome can lead to deeper connection. Using the biblical metaphor, perhaps insight that leads to healthy boundaries constitutes the "better clothes" that God provides for Adam and Eve.

Many who write about emotional defenses distinguish between "primitive" defenses and "mature" defenses. Primitive indicates that these defenses are often automatic and occur without full conscious awareness. Mature means that the defenses are more about intentional behaviors or actions people choose to protect themselves. For the purposes of this chapter, I will focus on a selection of more unconscious defenses and defensive behaviors because they tend to be disruptive to relationships and an internal sense of well-being. My goal is to identify key defensive behaviors that I have encountered frequently in my personal life and professional work. I hope to help you be able to identify them in yourself (or others) and to think about how these defenses are serving you (or not) and how you might begin to move to place of more openness.

Repression, Denial, Dissociation

Repression, denial, and dissociation are related but not the same. In general, we might think of repression and dissociation as responses to traumatic events. They reflect an internal attempt to separate one's conscious self, emotionally and mentally, from painful experiences or memories. In many cases, people who experience trauma, either once or recurring, find that their minds allow them to escape what is happening by sectioning off the traumatic experience from conscious awareness. In more severe cases, such as physical abuse and sexual assault or abuse, people may develop a completely different personality within them that carries the memory or experience for them, allowing another part of these people to function day to day without the burden of a difficult memory. In a less severe case, like in a family where there is regular fighting or drama, people might find that they regularly slip into fantasy (television, movies, books, video games) or fall into a "daze" or a "trance" to escape difficult situations. Both the more extreme and more mundane examples are types of dissociation. Once a person's mind has established this as a way to escape difficulty, it is easy for them to fall back into these states in other uncomfortable situations.

Repression is another response to traumatic, hurtful, confusing, or incongruent behaviors, but instead of dissociating from reality, people utilizing this defense have what seems like selective memory. The event and the experience of it are pushed out of conscious awareness, and people function as if these things are not part of their lives or histories. On the one hand, we can see how this might be beneficial since it allows people to continue their daily lives. On the other hand, however, if they experienced or witnessed this event, their repressed memories can affect them unconsciously and be expressed in several ways, including bad dreams, hypersensitivity to certain events or types of interactions, or irrational emotional responses. One example is a person who maintains positive memories of a parent or a partner by repressing memories of mistreatment in order to maintain a positive image of the other. In the case of a partner, a person might also repress memories of maltreatment in order to avoid examining why they allow themselves to be mistreated. If the repressed memory is of one's own behavior, they may keep the memory out of awareness to protect their image of themselves. The repressed memory may reflect an aspect that they would prefer not to confront or accept. An example is a person who insists that they were a good friend despite numerous times of hurtful or disappointing behavior. They are not lying; if the memories are repressed, they are reporting what they remember. Trying to talk to this person about their problematic behavior may be disorienting for them, and they may respond with defensive anger. This often leads to "gaslighting." This term refers to the phenomenon in which someone denies another person's experience or memory, leaving them feeling confused and questioning their own experience or sanity.

In both repression and dissociation, the hidden, separated aspects of self can come to conscious awareness in an environment of safety, but I believe an intentional course of therapy with a professional is most often required. Clients have come to me because formerly repressed memories of their past began to surface. Some have also come to me unaware of certain repressed memories only to have them brought to light as therapy deepens and we explore various aspects of the client's life in an environment of increasing safety.

Denial can be related or similar to repression, but it is different because denial can be conscious, unconscious, or semiconscious. Denial and repression are probably at the heart of most defensive responses and actions. A person can deny an event that has happened or an aspect of self that they don't want to admit. They may be aware that they are denying something because they cannot face the shame of admitting the truth, or they may unconsciously employ other defenses and behaviors to keep themselves from seeing what others more readily see in them. In either case, a person who is in denial about a particular issue will likely respond poorly to anyone who directly or indirectly points out the denied aspect. This response is an attempt to keep the attention somewhere else. Before I began my own therapy and started working on these things in myself, I was extremely sensitive to criticism. This sensitivity was driven by my insecurity, perfectionism, and desire to maintain a good public image. If I did something that suggested I might not be perfect, I avoided taking responsibility, refused conversations about the issue, and tried to move on as quickly as possible. People with similar experiences may also attack others for how or when they bring up a particular issue, but we should recognize that the attack is part of the defense.

Imagine you want to talk to a partner or a friend about something hurtful they did. You attempt to bring it up with them, but instead of looking at themselves and taking responsibility for their actions, they turn on you and say, "I can't believe you're bringing this up now" or "You are *so* sensitive." As noted above regarding "gaslighting," the person may also flatly deny that what you are bringing up even happened. The first two types of responses are designed to remove the focus from the person's behavior and put the focus on you. Examples of more gaslighting responses might be "That didn't happen" or "You're crazy."

As I began to work on myself in therapy, I often recognized feelings of shame in myself. I knew I was avoiding something. I began to think, "My old self would want to sweep this under the rug or avoid it, which means the healthy thing is probably the hard thing. I need to take responsibility for it, address it with an apology, [or whatever was needed]." Denial can be deeply rooted and difficult to overcome, but it is not impossible.

Projection, Introjection, and Mirrors

Projection (or projective identification) and introjection function in opposite ways to protect a person. In projection, people see the disowned parts of themselves in other people. As I understand this, it is often at the root of self-righteousness. If I see myself as righteous and perfect in keeping "the rules," then I may not be willing to look at my own jealousy, anger, sexual feelings, need to control, etc. Instead, I see these things in others and regularly accuse them of feeling those things instead. In a relationship, I might wonder why the other person is so angry or accuse them of being jealous when I am the one who feels those things; the feelings are ignored, repressed, or disavowed. In the Twelve Step tradition, one of their sayings is, "If you spot it, you got it." When we assume the worst of others or judge them for what we perceive as a particular feeling, thought, or behavior, it is often because we also struggle in that way. Again, this serves to keep the focus off our own struggles, but it is also a way of "projecting" what could be self-judgment onto others and judging them instead.

Projection also happens when we assume others judge us in the way that we judge ourselves. If a person is self-conscious about their income, they might make regular comments about money, how much things cost, or how much others flaunt their wealth, assuming that this is the first thing people will notice about them and a primary way of assessing others. This insecurity can also cause a person to misinterpret what people say because they read nefarious intent into potentially innocent comments. They are "projecting" their own self-judgment onto the other. I have had conversations with people who reported about their experience at work or at a party and said, "I can't believe everyone there was looking at me because of _____." In reality, if anyone noticed the object of insecurity, they probably did not give it a second thought. Because the person feels insecure or self-conscious about that particular thing, however, they assume everyone else also notices it.

Projective identification takes projection a step further. In this defense, the person being projected onto might assume the identity that the other person projects. Their willingness to believe or assume the projection is potentially a result of their own insecurity or their deference to the one who projects. A person who is insecure about their weight might make comments to someone else about the weight the other person has gained. If the other person then becomes insecure or begins focusing on appearance, the identity is successfully transferred. Similarly, a person engaged in secretive behavior might accuse a friend or partner of being insecure or suspicious because they ask questions. If the partner then begins to feel like they *are* too insecure or overly suspicious, the projection is internalized.

Introjection is related. In this defense, a person adopts the attributes of another as their own. This occurs as a normal part of development; children often "introject" their parents' views, values, attitudes, etc. In the course of normal development, we would hope that children mature, begin to explore their own identities, and adopt the parents' attributes by choice or discover something new that they feel fits them better. However, introjection can function as a defense in a couple of ways. First, a person who is insecure about their identity or lacks a good sense of self may adopt the ways of others to avoid the task of finding their own identity. Second, introjection also can serve to ease social anxiety. In what has also been called "twinning," a more anxious person might adopt the views of another in order to ease potential conflict between them: "You and I are the same. We like the same things; we agree on these big issues." A combination of these two presentations of introjection is also possible. Such adoption of views and values is not genuine, but it is also not consciously inauthentic. This defense strategy serves to protect the person from their fear of rejection.

There is a distinction between a conscious exploration of new ways of being and relating versus an unconscious adoption of others' affect. As I was developing personally and professionally, I often identified people around me who had traits or outlooks that I admired. I regularly sought time with them over coffee or a meal, asked how they developed such traits or views, and explored how they managed various aspects of their lives. I would then see if there were aspects of what was shared that I felt fit with the person that I wanted to be and try to emulate such things in my life. Some people might refer to this as "fake it till you make it." It is acting the way we want to be until it becomes a genuine part of who we are. The difference between this and introjection is the intentionality and personal adaptation as opposed to unconscious or semiconscious wholesale adoption of another's behavior, views, etc.

So how do we identify or know ourselves? We often know ourselves by the way others react and respond to us. This is known as "mirroring." When we interact with another person, their response to us and what they say to us reflect something about how we are perceived and give us clues to who we are. This is how an infant learns about feelings. The way a parent reacts to an event cues a child about how they should feel, or the way a parent reacts to a child's response to an event is a clue to whether the child's response is appropriate (by parental standards). As we have already seen, how others interact with us is influenced by a number of factors, some of which have more to do with the other person than with us. In that regard, not all mirrors are the same, and not all mirrors give us a trustworthy reflection of ourselves.

If a person is projecting their own insecurity and disowned parts onto us, their reflection of us may be more like a funhouse mirror. The image may look somewhat like us, but it is distorted by the other person's projection and does not appear to be accurate to us. We need people in our lives whom we trust to be honest in order to provide a more accurate reflection of who we are. The trustworthy people who know us can give us a true reflection of ourselves. When I was doing my Clinical Pastoral Education (chaplain training), part of our training was a group interaction called "interpersonal relationships" (IPR). In this group, we focused on our relationships with our fellow chaplain residents and dealt with issues of our personal interactions and professional identity in the training program. There were times when others might project their issues onto someone, but there were regular opportunities to gain insight as others offered feedback about us that came from our various interactions.

In IPR one week, we were to describe ourselves using an object. I don't recall the exact assignment, but I described myself as a "big teddy bear." I am big and a little "squishy," and I care about others and seek to be comforting. One of the other residents said that sometimes I can be like a "big grizzly bear." I was not sure I was ready to accept that, so I said I would "have to reflect on that." Part of "reflecting" meant going home and talking to my wife. My wife Lynda is a "mirror" that I trust. I told her about IPR that day and the grizzly bear comment. She looked at me and said, "Duh!" She observed that I am a big person with a big presence, and I can be quick with a comeback or a harsh comment at times, which is sometimes intimidating. I was shocked. Grizzly bear was not my idealized self-image. I was not sure I wanted to be seen that way. Over time, I realized I had to be aware that others sometimes experienced me as bigger than I feel, and some people see me as intimidating when I do not intend to be. I also learned that there are times when being big and intimating is not necessarily a bad thing.

In other experiences, I have had people accuse me of being this way or that. I try to be open to reflect on others' feedback and whether their reflected image of me bears resemblance to who I think I am, but I regularly go to the people I trust to get a better reflection of myself. "Is this me?" I might ask, and the answer is sometimes, "Well, you know you can be like this or that, but I would not identify you as that person did." Then I work on what I can and let go of what may not be mine to work on.

Reaction Formation

As a defense "reaction formation" is characterized by an irrational adoption of a particular outlook, value, or behavior that is a conscious, semiconscious, or unconscious reaction to something from the past that is not fully resolved. Classic examples are a person who grows up with an angry parent and vows to be upbeat and positive or, as noted in the previous chapter, a person who grows up with an alcoholic parent and vows never to touch alcohol (and probably keep others in their family from doing so with strict rules and hypervigilance). A similar example might be a person who grew up in a filthy home who vows to keep their house clean and neat by compulsively cleaning and forcing others to conform to rules of cleanliness. It might be a person who grew up in poverty and vows to work hard and make money so that they (and their family) do not have that experience.

You might recognize that not all such reactions are unhealthy and can be part of resilience that assists some to overcome a difficult history. However, the problematic aspect of such reactions is in the potential irrationality of the beliefs or feelings and the extremity of the behaviors. From the examples above, the child of an angry parent who insists on keeping things positive and happy might ignore or deny feelings of agitation or aggravation or irrationally attack agitation, aggravation, or anger in others. In this way, the denied or repressed feelings are expressed in passive-aggressive ways, and the person's behavior might be controlling as they try to manipulate situations for a particular outcome. Ironically, because such a person cannot completely control their feelings and responses, they could at times find themselves feeling or acting irrationally angry. They might then blame others or be overwhelmed with depression that they have failed to live up to the ideal they set for themselves.

A healthier version would be to reflect on their childhood experiences, identify the feelings they had growing up or the feelings about how they grew up, and work toward healthy expression of those feelings. This would allow them to have a wider range of emotional expression and learn how to express their feelings in more constructive ways.

Intellectualization, Acting Out, and Alligator Brain

Intellectualization is a way to avoid feelings by focusing on what seems "logical." There are benign and hurtful expressions of this defense. In therapy, I have worked with clients who identified a particular issue or behavior that they considered a problem. Some of them spent session after session reflecting on why this thing existed or why that thing happened. They read many books on how to overcome their issue or books on theories to explain a particular behavior. At times, I found such conversations enjoyable and intellectually stimulating. However, often these people spend so much time analyzing that they avoid the feelings and don't allow themselves to use their feelings as another resource for understanding themselves. People may dismiss feelings as irrelevant or problematic instead of looking to them as a source of wisdom that can help them understand how an event affected them or how a particular behavior might serve them. This is especially true if a person is aware that they would prefer not to deal with the unexamined feeling. For example, a person who has experienced a great loss is aware of deep sadness at some level and of the difficulty adjusting to the loss. However, they talk about grief as a hypothetical concept. They might read multiple books on loss and grief. They might wonder why they are not experiencing some of the feelings described in the book, or they might explore various activities designed to evoke feelings in a grieving person. A friend once talked about the loss of his parent. He said he knew the stages of grief and he could identify each one. In his mind, he checked them off and then thought, "Well, I have now grieved." But later the flood of feelings came as events evoked unexpressed grief. For a similar client, focusing more on their relationship with and memories of the person who is gone might help them connect to their feelings, moving them out of their head and into their actual experience.

Another example is someone who feels a feeling and is aware of it, but they judge and analyze it rather than just acknowledging the feeling. This is especially happens if a person is uncomfortable or confused by the feeling. Earlier I mentioned that during my time in psychoanalysis, my analyst would ask me about her being gone on vacation weeks before she left. In the exchange about this when I began to cry at the thought of her being gone, I felt so silly for feeling sad that I could not let myself be sad. With my analyst's help, once I accepted that I was sad, I was better able to reflect on what previous experiences were informing my feelings in the moment. As long as I judged the feeling as intellectually irrational, I could not experience the feeling or understand it. The possibility of change begins when we can accept what is. As long as we fight what is, we cannot do anything meaningful about it.

Intellectualization can also be more deeply ingrained in a person and can more profoundly affect their relationships. A person might adopt a particular belief system or set of values that they believe are logically superior to other ways of being. They seek to make decisions based on these beliefs and values, regularly discounting or disavowing anything that does not fit them. This discounting of other perspectives likely affects the way they respond to other people. A more straightforward example might be a Christian person who believes that "to walk by faith and not by sight" (2 Cor 5:7) means that we should not pay attention to our feelings but only focus on what we believe is objectively true. In a small group I led once, I talked about the value of emotions and what we can learn by paying attention to them. One participant in the class said firmly and sternly, "As Christians, we should not pay attention to feelings. We are to only follow God's word." If we read carefully, we will see that the Bible often mentions emotions, and the admonition seems to be that emotions are a natural expression of what we feel. While our emotions should not always dictate our behavior, they can teach us something of value.

The opposite of intellectualization may be what some call "acting out." There are at least two ways to think about this defense mechanism. The first is when a person has repressed certain feelings, either because they judge them as wrong or they are too uncomfortable, but then "acts out" these feelings unexpectedly. Often this acting out is displaced from the true object of the feelings to a target that feels safer. A person might feel angry at their boss at work but does not want to express their true feelings in the workplace, so they come home and are irritable with the kids or irrationally angry with the dog. A person might continue to behave in an angry way while denying they are angry. A person might behave in a sexually seductive way while not realizing or accepting that they are doing so. They are "acting out" the feelings but not identifying with them. Such feelings are generally not expressed in healthy ways or in ways the person acting out can even acknowledge.

Second is the concept of impulse control. Poor impulse control is a symptom of various psychiatric conditions. However, an emotionally immature person with repressed or disowned feelings may experience certain emotions at a powerful, overwhelming level. They may feel compelled to act on such emotions, not realizing that they have an option not to act on them. As one writer described it, "If we do not make the unconscious conscious, it will continue to control our lives and we will call it fate."[3] Some may feel justified in acting on such feeling because the feelings are so strong. Without reflection,

---

3. This quote is often misattributed to Carl Jung, who did write,

> The psychological rule says that when an inner situation is not made conscious, it happens outside, as fate. That is to say, when the individual remains undivided and does not become conscious of his inner opposite, the world must perforce act out the conflict and be torn into opposing halves. (*Collected Works of Carl Jung: Aion*, trans. R. F. C. Hull, ed. H. Read et al., 2nd ed., vol. 9, pt. 2 [Bollingen Series XX, Princeton: Princeton University Press, 1970], 70–71.)

these feelings might seem uncontrollable, even attributed to God or described as "meant to be." The person may say they cannot help themselves or control their behavior. This is often true when someone experiences a strong attraction for another person or, ironically, feels a strong dislike for another person (or group of people). In such a scenario, a person might say they cannot help acting on their feelings because they do not have the tools to manage otherwise. Such expression of strong feeling without impulse control is often damaging to relationships and can be experienced as frightening to oneself and others.

Helping such people move from experiencing their feelings to being more "in their head" can be helpful. One tools I have offered many clients over the years, especially around strong feelings of anger, is a reflection on what I call "Alligator Brain." People with more scientific sensibilities might refer to this as "reptilian brain," but I think making it specific to alligators is more fun and illustrative. Alligators have very small brains. They have just enough brain to get them around and manage the necessities of life. They are driven solely by instinct, impulse, and reaction. If an alligator is injured or threatened, it might bite you (fight), it might run (flight), or it might (at least temporarily) be paralyzed by fear (freeze). If you back an alligator into a corner and shake a stick in its face, it is likely to bite you. That is an instinctual reaction, not a calculated response. We all have a part of our brain that is like the alligator's; it is at the base of the brain in the brain stem. When we feel threatened or hurt, we can also respond by "biting" in our own way. The alligator part of our brains does not distinguish between emotional and physical pain. If we feel hurt or threatened by another person's actions or words, we are likely to respond by lashing out or reacting to protect ourselves. The perceived threat might also be about our idealized self-image. If, for example, I think of myself as a kind or responsible person, anything someone says or does that indicates I have been hurtful or irresponsible might evoke a strong emotional reaction. I experience a threat to my image of myself and am fearful of how others perceive me. In such an emotionally charged interaction, I might also feel the need to withdraw or flee.

What makes us different from the alligators is all the rest of our brain, the cerebral cortex. Alligators don't have this part of the brain. It gives us the ability to reflect on what is happening and choose how to respond instead of reacting instinctually. Sometimes our reactions are so quick that our developed brains can only help us after the fact to understand what we reacted to and why. However, there is a window of a fraction of a second between the impulse to react and acting in which we can interrupt the behavior. If we practice, we can develop a longer gap between the impulse and the response and choose how to act. In that tiny gap, there is an opportunity to dissect what is prompting our reaction. This requires growing in awareness of our own feelings in general and learning to identify feelings in the moment. I always add to this that *no one* ever gets this perfectly right, and no one can do it in every circumstance. Perfection in this is not the goal; the goal is progress.

As a person begins to practice this discipline of interrupting the impulse to react, they might not be able to stop the reaction at first. They might only notice that there was an opportunity to interrupt the reaction and then, after the fact, process the experience and precipitating feelings. Sometimes the ability to decipher what happened in a particular encounter will occur five minutes after the event. On other occasions, the time to process can be more like five hours or five days. Ultimately, there will be a chance to return to the one that prompted this reaction and offer an apology and our best understanding of what happened.

The way we reflect on our alligator response often relates to how we cope with anger. In Matthew 5:21-26, Jesus says a person who is angry with another person is subject to the same judgment as a person who murders. This teaching has led some people to believe that being angry is a sin. I think this reading of the passage is too casual. Also, Paul writes in Ephesians 4:26 to "Be angry, but do not sin." This teaching implies that feelings and actions are different. We can acknowledge the feeling of anger and choose how to express it. We are not to be governed by our feelings, but nor should we discount or ignore them.

The teachings of Jesus from Matthew 5 require more than a surface reading to understand. This section on anger comes in a series of teachings in which Jesus illustrates that he did not come to abolish the law of Moses but to fulfill it (v. 17). He also says our righteousness should exceed that of the Pharisees. Note that Jesus's interactions with the Pharisees always demonstrated that they were likely to focus on the letter of the law while disregarding the law's underlying principle of love. Jesus illustrates that truth in Matthew 5 by comparing the teachings from the law on adultery, murder, divorce, swearing oaths, and retaliation to a higher calling that takes seriously the underlying principle for each teaching. Jesus's fulfillment of the law here is rich, and each statement is worthy of reflection, but for now let's focus on murder and anger.

Jesus notes that the letter of the law says not to take another person's life: "You have heard it said . . . you shall not murder." While most people find it easy to refrain from murdering, Jesus expands on the idea, saying that if you are angry with your brother or sister, you are liable to judgment. This is why many people draw the conclusion that simply being angry is a sin. But notice that Jesus describes what the expression of anger might look like. He says insulting another person is worthy of judgment by the council, and calling someone a fool is worthy of hell. Jesus then instructs his hearers that if they are in the act of worship offering a sacrifice, and they realize that someone has something against them, they should leave their gift and go be reconciled to their brother or sister.

Reflect on the reasons a person might murder another person. I will not cover every possible reason, but generally the murderer is driven by their "alligator brain" emotion of unbridled rage. This person has deep hatred or disgust for someone else or shows no regard for another person as try to steal from them or cover their own shame about a wrongdoing. These feelings involve a depersonalization of the other person. The angry one is so wrapped up in their own perspective, judgment, or selfish desires that they lose sight of the human being before them.

Jesus describes anger that discounts the humanity of another person. Calling someone a fool or idiot is discounting them as a human being. As I read this, to be angry enough with someone to insult them is to be driven by one's emotions to the point of rejecting their humanity. The roots of murder lie in the slow erosion of the ability to see someone else as child of God worthy of love. Later in Matthew 5, Jesus talks about learning to love our enemies. We must strive to see every other person, even someone we perceive as an enemy, as a human being. We may not agree with them, but if we reduce them to something less than human, the seeds of hatred and murder are sown.

Jesus's admonition to leave our gift at the altar demonstrates that our love of God is intimately connected to our relationship with others. Notice that Jesus says if you realize *the other person has something against you*. This means being aware that we may have done something to another person to cause harm or alienate them. The *feeling* of anger is not the sin. What is problematic is an unbridled anger, which leads to hurtful insults and actions and alienates others. This is why Paul says later that we are to be angry but not sin. The feeling is not the sin; the inability to pay attention to the feeling and learn how to express it appropriately is the sin.

In his book, *Voice of the Heart*, Chip Dodd says paying attention to our anger can show us the things we are most passionate about. This perspective allows us to reflect on what causes us to feel angry. The angry feelings might point us to people who are important to us and may reveal insecurities in ourselves as we recognize that certain words or interactions evoke those feelings. Exploring what matters to use can also help us identify social issues and injustices in the world that touch us deeply.

Other people talk about anger as a "secondary emotion"— a feeling expressed when another feeling is present that might cause us to feel more vulnerable. There are certain feelings of anger, especially around issues of justice or fairness, that I might think of as "primary anger." This involves the recognition that something is not right, and the strong feeling motivates us to action. Like the alligator, however, if we feel threatened or hurt, we might respond with anger. Anger can protect us from recognizing an underlying threat, or anger might be a large reaction (like an alligator bite) designed to keep people at a safer distance. The big, angry responses might also be a form of projection where we seek to inflict a wound on someone else that gives them an experience of the pain they inflicted on us. In such scenarios, the pain, hurt, betrayal, threat to our self-image, or physical threat of harm evokes the secondary emotional response of anger. A healthier conversation requires identifying the underlying primary emotion(s) and giving a voice to that. This is difficult because sharing deeper feelings often feels more vulnerable. And there are certainly times when other people are not safe, emotionally or physically, and sharing deep emotions only makes us more vulnerable to abuse. We must choose wisely when to be vulnerable, but in some cases, the vulnerability of sharing underlying emotions can help disarm a conflict and create an opportunity for a better conversation.

Passive Aggression & Manipulation

Some forms of aggression are big and frightening. Strong physical, verbal, or emotional actions can achieve manipulation and control. However, people also express anger in more passive ways. As we have already seen, some in the Christian community (and outside it) may see anger as bad and undesirable. In our culture, women are often raised to be "good girls" or "nice ladies" who do not demonstrate strong emotions, especially anger. Sadly, men are often enculturated to see things like sadness or disappointment as weakness and are left with anger as the only option to express emotion.

If a person wants to avoid expressing or acknowledging anger, they might behave in a way, intentionally or unintentionally, to get what they want or avoid doing what they do not want by acting contrary to the desired behavior or outcome. Such a person might deny their anger while behaving in inflammatory ways. The level can range from a mundane scenario in which they avoid doing something asked of them in order to exercise a sense of control to a moment when they act in a passive aggressive manner if they feel unable to engage potential conflict about the issue at hand. Avoiding conflict in order to maintain an image of good relationships or to resist uncomfortable conversations is a predominant reason for passive aggression in relationships.

Another way of attempting to avoid conflict or feelings of vulnerability is through control and manipulation. A passive aggressive conflict-avoidant person might have a desired outcome for a particular situation but not feel comfortable expressing their desire or opinion. Instead, they might try to arrange a situation or drop hints to get the desired outcome without a big confrontation or the vulnerability of wanting or needing something from another person.

In 2010, my family lived with my mother and her husband after we lost our house to a mudslide during the flood in Nashville that year. One day at breakfast, my mother told me she planned to have a local company come to help move a large piece of furniture in her home. I heard her words and said, "Ok. That sounds good." A couple of days later, my mother posted on social media, "Frustrated that I can't get anyone to help me move [said piece of furniture]." I confronted my mother and observed that she had never asked me for help; she had simply told me her plans to get the project done. My mom did not like conflict, and she did not like to ask for help. I think she hoped that telling me about hiring the local company would prompt me to volunteer to help her without her having to ask.

Of course, attempts at controlling outcomes can be more sinister. One person's attempt to control the actions of another through verbal or physical intimidation has many possible motivations. However, a major one is related to fear. If a person does not know how to deal with vulnerability or is extremely insecure, they might project their fears onto someone close to them and behave as if the person is a threat, when the threat is more in their own mind.

A classic example is a boyfriend or husband without the emotional vocabulary to express himself and possibly without the emotional awareness to understand his own feelings who attempts to control his significant other in order to ease his own anxiety. If he is insecure that his partner might leave him for someone else, he might try to control where the partner goes or who they spend time with in order to limit his sense of risk. This extreme example is unfortunately all too real for many people. But more mundane versions exist. The bottom line is that one person tries to control another person's thoughts, feelings, or behaviors in order to avoid facing a particular feeling within themselves.

As a younger person, I read 1 Corinthians 13:4, learned that "love does not insist on its own way," and thought it meant I should always defer to others. When I got married, I thought this meant I should defer to my wife in everything. She should pick the restaurants, the movies, and the vacation spots. I thought I should let her determine just about anything. I also wrote off things I liked that my wife did not like, and I felt that I had to try to like everything she liked. This turned out to be a terrible interpretation of 1 Corinthians 13:4, and it did not make a happy marriage for either of us.

I have come to believe that "Love does not insist on its own way" is less about always deferring to my partner and more about not trying to control my partner's behavior so that I can feel comfortable. If she wants to try something new or do something different, I should not try to dissuade her because of my fears about what it means for me or our relationship. I want her to be all that God created her to be. If I have feelings about her trying new things, I need to work on myself and my feelings, not try to change or control her. I need to learn how to manage myself and not try to manage her. I think the same logic applies to all relationships.

Magical Thinking, Wishful Thinking & the Illusion of Control

The attempt to have a sense of control over a situation is not limited to manipulation or passive aggression. Some people avoid the difficult feeling of lack of control by unconsciously adopting an elaborate system of beliefs, thoughts, or superstitions that help them ignore the reality that we cannot control everything. These beliefs, etc. can also contribute to avoiding responsibility for their own actions. If a person believes that God will provide or God will change things, they might believe they do not have to do anything or take any risks. (Ironically, they may feel anger later if God does not provide in the way they expect.) Other magical thinking might simply be denial. A person might believe that a hurtful friend or abusive partner will somehow change despite no evidence to support that belief. A person might also maintain a sense of control through superstitions or particular religious practices. Those who believe that if they live a certain way, pray a certain way, or repeat certain rituals they will get a desired outcome can maintain a sense of control in situations that feel out of control. However, in such cases people might be vulnerable to feelings of disappointment when the desired outcome does not happen.

Many people do not realize that they carry such beliefs until the beliefs fail them. A person may not consciously profess that "being a good person" will bring good luck to them or that following the guidelines of the Bible will result in the avoidance of difficulty. But when tragedy befalls the person, their underlying beliefs are often exposed. As they sit in my therapy office, they might say for the first time ever, "This was not supposed to happen. I have been a good person." The statement reveals a practice of faith or belief that outcomes can be changed or tragedy avoided by doing or saying the right thing. Sometimes, that is just not true.

Conversion and Somatization

Conversion and somatization are technically different experiences, but the terms are often used interchangeably. These experiences are probably the hardest to understand and the most resistant to psychotherapeutic treatment. In both experiences, a suppressed or denied conflict or feeling is transformed into physical symptoms. We might understand that a person with a great deal of anxiety or depression would begin to experience fatigue, increased heart rate, or increased blood pressure. The emotional state is related to and intricately connected to the body's biochemical reactions, and if a person is triggered in a certain way, the physical body can begin to feel the symptoms. Deep sadness can be experienced as literal pain in the heart. Anxiety can manifest as tingling in the extremities, rapid breathing, or a racing heartbeat. Somatization is generally a physical manifestation of conscious or unconscious feelings. Many people are aware of and focus on the physical symptoms, often without recognizing the underlying emotional dynamic.

When our daughter was in middle school, she moved to a new school. She began to develop "stomachaches" and sometimes missed school. We took her to the doctor. The doctor was concerned about possible diagnoses, and we discussed treatment options. My daughter's symptoms were very real, and she had physical pain. However, we learned that she was also having conflict with a particular teacher who seemed to single her out in class in ways that felt cruel or humiliating to our daughter. When we addressed the classroom issue, the physical symptoms subsided. In such scenarios, it can be easy to ignore the environmental, relational, and emotional aspects of physical symptoms because there are often straightforward treatments for physical ailments, while emotional and relational issues are more complicated. Paying attention to somatic symptoms like breath, heart rate, etc. can be a way to begin exploring (and treating) emotional issues. Think, for example, of how meditation (a body practice) can bring increased relaxation, focus, and a sense of well-being.

Conversion can be more complicated in that the unresolved issues can result in physical symptoms, but often the physical symptoms do not have an identifiable physiological cause. This occurs when the repressed conflict, feelings, etc. result in physical conditions. With a somaticized symptom, paying attention to the physical experience might help point toward a helpful treatment or recognize the possible link between emotional state and symptoms. In a conversion experience, the connection between the physical symptoms and the repressed experience or feelings is not immediately clear or easily discernable.

The connection between physical symptoms and emotional well-being is not always discernable and can make these symptoms difficult to treat. A person with deeply repressed experiences or feelings might overly invest in their physical symptoms and reject any possible connection to their emotional well-being. In this case, any attempt at psychotherapeutic work that attempts to connect emotional state to symptoms is summarily rejected. The person's symptoms are very real, and they are not readily willing to consider nonphysical treatment. For many, offering such treatment can feel insulting. And it is true that there is a history of women receiving less than good medical care because their symptoms were too quickly attributed to "hysteria." Finding the balance between physical symptoms caused by emotional distress or repressed experience and a true physiological condition is challenging, and this is one reason that I regularly encourage my clients to receive a full physical before proceeding with therapy. I don't want to try to treat an "emotional problem" that is a thyroid condition, and I don't want to assume only a physical problem when there is a deep and unresolved personal issue.

Withdrawal & Humor

When emotions feel too big or interactions with others feel overwhelming, many people cope by withdrawing emotionally or physically leaving. Sometimes a friend literally leaves when feelings get too deep or scary for their comfort. Or a person wants to leave in the middle of an argument because they are flooded with emotions and cannot figure out how to manage their feelings and respond appropriately. Sometimes the "alligator brain" ignites a "fleeing" response rather than "fighting." Withdrawal can also take the form of substance abuse or overinvolvement in activities (including church and other "good things"). Using such behaviors and substances allows a person to avoid an uncomfortable feeling or situation. It can be difficult to challenge such behaviors because things like church or exercise are not generally considered bad.

Humor is another way that people avoid dealing directly with issues. A quick joke can deflect a potentially hurtful or inflammatory comment. Making a humorous comment about oneself or a situation can help a person switch away from a difficult topic or derail a conversation. Humor can be used in a passive-aggressive way when someone makes a joke but never has a real conversation about the topic. Humor can be used in many unhealthy ways, including sarcasm and veiled insults. However, for a person who is more emotionally healthy and personally aware, humor can be a healthy tool for diffusing a potentially difficult situation or acknowledging a hard truth.

Summary

"Defenses" help protect us from seeing and experiencing hard things within ourselves and help us feel emotionally safe from others. But these defenses keep us isolated from ourselves, others, and God. It has been my experience that the more emotionally immature or unhealthy a person is, the more likely they are to utilize many of these defenses. A person might use one defense more regularly than others, but it is common for someone to engage in various defenses at different times.

The defenses identified in this chapter do not represent all possible problematic behaviors. Many argumentative strategies are unconsciously deployed to help someone avoid having difficult conversations or taking personal responsibility. Trying to engage in a meaningful or difficult discussion with a person utilizing one or more defenses can seem futile since the conversations are often circular. They never lead to more depth or resolution. It can be hard to make a meaningful connection with someone who is heavily defended by such strategies. Some friendships are limited in potential for depth by people's inability to overcome their own defenses. This does not mean spending time with such people is always unpleasant, but there are limits to the level of possible connection.

Chapter 5

Healthy Interactions & Cultivating Trust

Becoming aware of our defensive strategies and striving to be more conscious of our internal world is a good beginning for emotional and relational health. As we grow more self-aware, we can be more self-revealing and make better connections with others. However, simply being aware of our own defenses does not necessarily mean that alternative healthy behaviors and attitudes are obvious. Many people grow up without adequate examples of emotional health and do not know how to create healthy relationships with others. A person might be aware that they do not want to be like a parent in one way or another, but they may not automatically identify the healthy alternative. This is where the reaction formation is problematic for some people. A person may consciously or unconsciously assume a behavior or affect that they believe is the opposite of a parent's problematic behavior but then hold that new behavior too rigidly and in an unhealthy manner. In this case, it is not corrective for them or for those around them and may create a related but different set of problems. Sometimes we need help identifying the healthy behaviors that help us avoid repeating the challenges of our past.

A common stereotype is that therapists want to dig into your past and blame your parents for your problems. This is rarely the case. First, some types of therapy do not explore a person's past at all. For those that do, it is important to realize that exploring one's past to understand the effects of family dynamics and childhood experiences is not an exercise in blame. As we saw in the last chapter, blaming is a defensive victim mentality that keeps us emotionally and relationally stuck. I have known people who have done enough therapy to understand how they were affected by their childhood environment and then stopped going to the therapist. They spend the rest of their lives blaming others for their lack of success or progress and making excuses for poor behavior and bad choices. This is *not* the goal of good psychotherapy. Insight should point us in the direction of vulnerabilities and indicate areas for work and growth. Many people also fear reflecting on the past because they long to hold a positive view of their parents, and they fear that deeper reflection on their parents' frailties will make mom and dad look bad. Good reflection on the past is not about blame but about understanding. While taking stock of how our past affects us is important, the ultimate result should be a greater appreciation for the complexity of our parents and ourselves. Rigid good or bad, black or white thinking is also a defense that guards against dealing with nuances of intrapersonal and interpersonal dynamics.

In her book *Adult Children of Emotionally Immature Parents*, Lindsey Gibson describes a variety of ways that "emotional immaturity" is present in families. Gibson does not limit emotional immaturity to one type of presentation (personality disordered, substance abuser, mentally ill, etc.) but instead captures these along with more mundane or subtle reactions and behaviors. None of us are completely emotionally healthy, and we will never be. We can strive for that goal, but we must appreciate progress over perfection. As the Apostle Paul wrote, "forgetting what lies behind and straining forward to what lies ahead, I press on toward the goal, toward the prize of the heavenly call of God in Christ Jesus. Let those of us, then, who are mature think this way, and if you think differently about anything, this, too, God will reveal to you" (Phil 3:13b-15). Many have interpreted the words "forget what lies behind" to mean "ignore what lies behind." But we need to take stock of our past, honor the ways we have been blessed and hurt, inventory our gifts and growing edges, and allow ourselves to feel whatever feelings are present before we can truly move on to a more mature and healthy way of being. There is no shortcut for this process.

The personal inventory process will hopefully help us recognize when we have a limited number of tools in our emotional toolbox.

Then we can identify what we need so we can press on toward the goal of emotional health. I have jokingly said to clients, "You can build a house with a hammer and a screwdriver, but that house is probably going to suck" (or more politely, "be uninhabitable"). In order to build a better house, we need a full box of tools so that we can complete the various tasks necessary. There are some "tools"—qualities, characteristics, and behaviors—that build better relationships. Part of a therapist's job is to assist clients in identifying which tools they need and to help them cultivate the new tools in their lives. Friends can also help identify possible parts of us in need of work and can help us practice new skills. In this chapter, I will identify some of the characteristics and skills that help build healthier, more trusting relationships.

Rule Number One: Show Up & Be as Honest as Possible

When sitting with a new psychotherapy client, I often explain my process of therapy. Among other things that I share, I tell them that their role in therapy is first to "show up" and second to "be as honest as possible" about themselves. I tell them I will do my best to create an environment that feels safe and that it is my job to listen as they share so I can help them understand more about themselves and identify the themes that run through the various things we discuss. For a person who has struggled with shame and used a number of defenses to keep others at a distance, being fully honest is challenging. This is particularly true for a person who has become so invested in their defenses that they do not know the full truth of who they are. The thought of showing up and being honest frightens them. A therapist friend once said, "I always trust that my clients are as honest with me as they can be; I just don't always trust that they know all there is to know about themselves." I would agree with this because I know it was true for me when I began therapy for myself. This is why creating an emotionally safe environment in therapy is critically important. Clients need a safe space to be honest and to learn about themselves.

For friends, the same rules can be true, and each person in the friendship must embody the expectations of both "therapist" and "client": showing up and being honest and creating the safe space to do that. As stated previously, the process of psychotherapy is designed to benefit one of the participants (the client). Friendship should be a relationship of mutuality in which both people seek to be open and create a safe space. In a friendship, any given conversation might focus more on the needs of one friend. However, in healthy friendships there is fluidity and mutuality. At a fundamental level, being open and honest with oneself first and then with another trusted person is the foundation of healthy interactions.

"Showing up" might seem like a self-evident aspect of therapy and friendship, but there are times when it is not. In the therapeutic process, some clients who are new to therapy envision meeting with me once a month. It has been my experience, as a client and the therapist, that the therapeutic process works better with meetings at more regular intervals. My preference for someone beginning therapy is to meet weekly. This facilitates the process of getting to know one another and keeps the thoughts and reflections from each session fresh in our minds. Contrary to many misconceptions, "the work" of psychotherapy does not only occur in the therapist's office; it also happens in the reflections and actions of the client between sessions. A person who shows up regularly for sessions but does not attempt to make any changes or implement new tools outside of therapy will not make much progress. As therapy progresses and a client practices new tools and new understanding, we might begin to meet less frequently but generally never less than every other week. (I am aware that other therapists have different ideas and modalities of therapy that would not follow the same patterns and recommendations that I make.)

Similarly, friendships take time. I get busy and do not always make time to visit with my friends. I have regular times set aside to spend with certain people, but there are others whom I greatly enjoy, and I am not always the first to make sure we meet. Without regular contact, friendships can lose momentum in the same way that therapy can. Meeting with friends does not need to be regimented or happen as regularly as therapy, but it does require time and intentionality. Many of us have some friends whom we may not see for a while, we seem to pick right back up where we left off whenever we get together. These are usually friends with a strong relational foundation. Regular contact is important for establishing and maintaining relationships, and being consistent in contact adds to the atmosphere that nurtures trust.

Be Curious & Open

In addition to "showing up and being honest," I think working to be more curious about yourself and being open to new ideas, insights, and ways of being are the next most critical aspects of good therapy and healthy interaction. In psychotherapy, clients are often in challenging circumstances because they have tried to solve their problems with the same set of tools and limited insight that contributed to creating the problem. They have worked hard with their "hammer and screwdriver" to build that house without realizing their tools are limited. Sadly, many people believe that because their hard work with their limited tools or insights has failed them, they are a failure for seeking help. It can be difficult to see beyond personal limitations. Some people get fixated on only one outcome that they think will fix their situation. Others believe that they have done all they can do but don't realize their resources are limited. Still others are so anxious about what therapy might bring up that they try to control the process. I once saw a couple for therapy who wanted to work on their relationship. They were both in their second marriage. When we talked about doing histories for each of them, I mentioned that we would discuss their history of relationships, including their previous marriages. They reacted strongly to my suggestion and told me they had agreed never to talk about their previous relationships with each other. They chose not to participate in therapy that involved such discussions. I regularly talk about doing a family history with clients and hear something like, "I don't see how that is going to be helpful." Sometimes they lack understanding of the process and how it can be helpful, but they may also fear what might be discovered if a full history is taken. In the face of discomfort and fears, asking for help invites new possibilities and is a great sign of health, strength, and courage. Part of growing is learning to be curious about yourself and about different ways of understanding events, other people, and yourself. Trusting a challenging process can often lead to insight that opens new possibilities.

Being open and curious also means that we are receptive to others' constructive feedback for us. People who are at least somewhat emotionally healthy might be able to see things in us that we cannot see ourselves. A trusting relationship provides opportunities for someone to offer observations or ask gentle, probing questions to assist us in self-discovery. We do not have to accept everything that another person offers us, but it can be helpful to reflect on the feedback received and assess whether we believe it needs our attention. Emotionally *unhealthy* people may also offer us feedback that they believe is accurate and warranted, but theirs is often self-serving and reflects more about them than it does about us. Being open, curious, and self-aware in the context of *relationships that we trust* is the best way to process the feedback of others and evaluate its merit. Finding that someone's feedback resonates with us, whether comfortable or uncomfortable, helps build trust with the person who offers it, while feedback that feels aggressive and defensive responses (our own or from the other person) negatively affect trust in a relationship.

Being curious about others is also a much better way to approach the world than assuming others are wrong or bad. When a person has different traditions, different customs, different ways of thinking, or any other differences, rather than assuming your way is the standard and the other way is wrong, it can be enlightening and uniting to be curious about how they see or do things. Currently, many places in the United States are involved in attempts to ban certain books and to limit what history can be taught in schools. It might be better to be curious about others' perspectives and about different ways of understanding. Remaining curious and open to learning new things might feel scary at times, but it can also lead to wonderful opportunities and insights. The fact that another person does something different does not mean our way is wrong, and the fact that someone thinks or believes something different should not feel like a challenge to our own beliefs. We can use this as a chance to engage in good dialogue and come to a new or better understanding of why we believe as we do. Either way, we must strive not to feel threatened when learning something new or hearing other perspectives. Having someone be curious about our views and willing to understand our perspective is an important aspect of establishing trust in a relationship. We should offer that to others as well.

Rule Number Three: Direct Communication

Beyond being open and honest in our communication, being "direct" is a critical element of healthy interactions. Being direct can indicate that we speak directly to another person (as opposed to talking about them), or it can mean that we speak plainly about what we mean. Both are sometimes uncomfortable, but they are critical to healthy interactions. Paradoxically, people regularly avoid these aspects of communication, believing that they are creating better relationships without conflict, but they rarely accomplish the goal with that strategy.

The concept of speaking directly to a person is probably best understood in the context of what are known as emotional or relational triangles. A relationship between two people functions much like a bicycle; it is stable while it functions normally. However, when a relationship becomes strained due to conflict or misunderstanding, is normal for people to "triangle" a third party to bring stability, like a third wheel on a tricycle. A person in conflict with another might reach out to a third person and talk about what has happened and how they feel. Ideally, the third person would provide feedback and perspective that helps the original person return to the friend to work things out so the relationship can return to its previous state. The third party might even function as a temporary intermediary to facilitate a restorative connection between the original people.

In unhealthy situations, the third party might be coerced into being an intermediary more permanently, and the dynamic can become fixed over time. A mother who has concerns about one child might implore another child to reach out to their sibling to check on them rather than directly communicating with the child who concerns her. In some families, certain members of the family may only talk to one other member of the family so that others only know about that one member through the person who keeps in contact with them. In some families, one parent may not communicate well with the children, but the other parent is in regular contact. In such families, there is not a direct relationship with the less communicative parent, and the relationship that exists is largely facilitated by the other parent who serves as the point of the triangle. In an unhealthy family, a parent might say to a child, "Let's go get some new clothes or ice cream but not tell the other parent." Consciously or unconsciously, this type of interaction is designed to build an alliance between the parent and child and can undermine the relationship between the two parents.

In friendships, two friends may have a disagreement, and another friend insinuates themselves into the conflict with the stated goal of repairing it by going between the two who are arguing. Again, this not unhealthy if the original relationship is restored, but some people thrive on the drama of conflict by serving as a go-between and keeping the conflict going. It could also be that two people regularly talk about another friend (or another person) rather than having direct communication and connection with the person they talk about. Often such arrangements among friends are strategic, designed to create alliances and establish power differences among the "friends." One friend sharing information about another to a third person can be designed to create a bond, but the bond comes at the expense of the one who is discussed.

In Murray Bowen's family systems theory, one hallmark of relational health is direct communication between each person and every other person in a particular family or system. Bowen wrote about his own experience of sending letters to each member of his family in which he shared secrets and broke historic family alliances designed to maintain power among some while keeping others in a disadvantaged position. He said that when he announced he would no longer be triangled in certain family relationships and intended to avoid keeping secrets in order to have open, honest, and direct communication with each member of his family, some of them were angry that he was breaking the implied rules. Some of them made threats or attempted to emotionally manipulate him into changing his position. We might think of this as the relational equivalent of Isaac Newton's Third Law: "For every action, there is an equal and opposite reaction." Sometimes referred to as a "change-back reaction," the response of others in the system when one of them attempts to establish healthier boundaries and interactions is often threats (emotional or physical), bargaining, or rejection in an attempt to bring the person back to their expected role or previous functioning in the system. Being honest and direct in communication and seeking to avoid secrets, triangles, and alliances can be difficult and sometimes unpopular, but it leads to healthier relationships and less anxiety for the person who trying to manage the delicate balance of interactions and allegiances. If a person can persist in direct, open, and honest communication, the system will often adjust to a new normal. However, sometimes the new normal means excluding the one who wishes to change and allowing the system to return to unhealthier interactions without disruption.

In addition to the avoidance of speaking directly with others, another aspect of unhealthy communication is a lack of clarity. While there are examples of people who utilize lack of clarity to manipulate others and gain an advantage from the ambiguity, most people who lack clarity in communication do so for less nefarious purposes, generally to avoid conflict or to avoid hurting another person. Others may avoid clear communication so they do not have to take responsibility for their actions or face the consequences of something they have done.

Many years ago, Lynda and I had friends who referred to potential difficulties in their marriage as "lamp issues." This stemmed from an event early in their marriage in which they shopped for furnishings for their home. In a store, the husband saw a lamp that was interesting to him and pointed it out to his wife. Thinking that he liked it, she said that she liked it. The husband questioned her, and because the wife said she liked it, the husband offered to buy it. The wife agreed because the husband seemed enthusiastic about buying the lamp. Sometime later, they discovered in a conversation that neither of them liked the lamp, but because they did not want to hurt the other's feelings, they had been dishonest. Being honest about our likes and dislikes, preferences, desires, dreams, beliefs, and limitations can sometimes make for strained or difficult conversation. However, being honest helps us avoid situations like "the lamp incident" and can facilitate deeper relationships.

As I described previously, early in my own marriage, I believed that harmony was the key to a good relationship. I regularly—consciously and unconsciously—agreed to do things with my wife that I did not want to do. I also did not suggest things I wanted to do because I knew she did not want to do them. This was evident in the classic conversations about where we would eat.

Where do you want to go eat?

Wherever you want to go is fine.

Do you have any suggestions?

I'm happy with whatever you want.

After a few years of marriage, it was clear that deferring to my wife was not the magic path to a happy marriage, and something needed to change. Thank goodness for good marriage counselors! Eventually, we learned how to express our desires, make suggestions, and be flexible with each other's tastes in the moment.

Years ago, I was in an ethics training program provided by the Tennessee Association of Pastoral Therapists. The presenter was the woman who had previously been my psychoanalyst. It was odd seeing her in this context, like seeing your first-grade teacher at the grocery store. But I quickly adapted to this new perception of her, and in her presentation, she made a comment that has stayed with me over the years. She said, "Never agree to do for a client what might cause you to resent them." As previously stated, objectivity is not the only component that makes psychotherapy therapeutic, but it is a critical element of the therapeutic relationship. If we agree to do something for a particular client that we don't want to do, the resulting resentment will affect our objectivity. At the time, I was regularly seeing clients until nine p.m. because they said it was the only time they could be seen. However, I realized that I did not want to be at work that late and that those clients were not getting my best because I harbored quiet resentment for being at the office into the night. Another example relates to fees for therapy. Back then I worked for a nonprofit organization that allowed me to see clients on a sliding scale without affecting my pay, but for most therapists in private practice, reducing someone's fee means losing money. Many therapists I know are willing to work with some clients on their fee but cannot adjust it for every single client. Adjusting my fee when I knew I could not afford to would require doing something for a client that might cause me to resent them. I have had clients ask if I could extend my time with them or do a favor for them outside of therapy. If I agree to do such things when I don't feel comfortable doing them, the seed of resentment is planted. In other cases, I could be putting myself at risk legally or ethically to try to accommodate such requests. I began to stop taking my last client at eight p.m. I began to hold the frame of therapy a little tighter than I had previously, and I became aware that what I learned in ethics training was good advice not only for doing therapy but also for doing life.

I realized that I had agreed to do some things in my own life because I felt guilty or pressured. I did them and then felt miserable and maybe even resentful at the person who had "manipulated me" into doing whatever it was. After that training, I began to realize that I had the power to say "no." There were times when I still said "yes" because I felt it was important, even though I did not want to. In those moments, I realized that I made the decision based on my own priorities because I had the power to say "no" but chose to say "yes." I felt more empowered. I became less a victim of others' wishes and felt more in control of myself. I have come to believe that this is at least part of the reason Jesus encouraged his followers not to swear an oath but simply to let their yes be yes and their no be no (Matt 5:36-37).

I worked as a hospital chaplain when I was training in pastoral psychotherapy. I was not paid directly for the hours of counseling I did for training, so I tried to help my family make ends meet by doing what I could. At one point, I was doing counseling and training, working as a part-time and on-call chaplain, and delivering pizzas.

I even agreed to take other chaplains' on-call shifts to try to make additional money. This meant spending the night in the hospital on a Friday or Saturday night. It was too much, and I was gone from home too often. My wife Lynda started complaining, and I agreed that I needed to cut back. Lynda and I wanted a night to be at home and watch TV together without other obligations. The week we talked about this, a hospital chaplain called and asked if I could cover an on-call shift for them on Friday so they could attend an event they had forgotten about. I said, "Oh, I am so sorry. I have other plans that night. I won't be able to cover for you, but I hope you can find someone." I hung up the phone, and Lynda, who had overheard this exchange, glared disbelievingly at me and asked angrily, "What plans do you have Friday night?" I said, "Lynda, my plans are to be right here with you on the sofa on Friday night." My "no" was still no, but I did not need to explain all the reasons for saying no or what I would be doing instead. I simply said, "I am sorry. I can't." This skill is often necessary to avoid putting myself in situations where I might resent someone.

Related to this concept of yes and no is the issue of oaths and truth-telling. I have seen people who were eventually determined to be guilty of something "swear on their mother's grave" that they were telling the truth. First, I think we should know how that person felt about their mother before proceeding, but the big gesture of swearing to be truthful is often just for show. As Jesus says in Matthew 5, we can simply tell the truth and let our yes be yes and our no be no. This might mean taking responsibility for our own actions and living with the consequences of what we have done. However, this might also mean creating difficulty for someone when we admit that yes, the person did such and such. We must realize that in these instances we do not create consequences for others; we simply allow them to experience the natural consequences of their own actions. No matter how many times a person might say, "I can't believe you did that to me," the reality is that we did not do anything but allow them to experience the results of their own actions.

Being clear, direct, and honest in communication is not always easy, but we feel more in control of our lives, experience less resentment and anger, and have clearer consciences when our communication follows these rules. Remember that part of being direct in our communication is making sure we understand others and asking for clarity when we are not sure what they mean.

Rule Number Four:
Seek Clarification

The lack of clear, direct communication from someone can lead us to situations where we act on faulty information, agree to things we did not understand, or accept "explanations" that do not make sense to us. In basic communication theory, the breakdown in communication is either because of a faulty transmission of the message, a bad receiver, or interference in the transmission. Think of a radio station. If the station puts out a signal that is too weak, it will not reach its intended audience. And if we as the audience do not have a proper receiver or a good enough antenna, we will not be able to pick up a signal no matter how strong and clear it is. Sometimes, though, electrical currents, storms, or metal objects around us cause interference in the signal. The transmission is strong and clear and our receiver works, but something interferes or degrades the signal between transmission and reception. Direct, open, honest communication makes for good transmission of a message, but not everyone is capable or willing to engage in such communication. There can also be gaps in information and our own interpretations that distort the received message or create interference. What can we do to improve the transmission and reception process?

John Savage recognizes five styles of communication that he identifies as (1) direct and open, (2) open but partial, (3) distorted full information, (4) distorted and deleted information, and (5) nonverbal communication (15–16). Direct and open communications happens when each party shares in the ways described above. Open but partial is when key information is intentionally or unintentionally left out. The listener must figure out the missing information or act on the information assuming that it is complete. Distorted full information occurs when the communicator seems to communicate openly, but there are intended or unintended distortions of reality that the listener may or may not be aware of. Distorted and deleted information is a more severe combination of partial and distorted in which the listener must do more work to decipher what is intended. As you can probably guess, nonverbal communication is when a person does not use words but simply behaves in ways that they hope will share something of their experience or feelings without any real clarification.

Except for direct and open, these communication types reflect faults in transmission. The listener is not getting a strong signal, and even if they listen well, the message is unclear and incomplete. The easiest way to deal with this is to ask for clarification. "When you say _____, I am not sure what you mean. Can you explain that?" We can also offer a report of our initial interpretation: "When you say _____, what I hear is _____." In such cases, we invite the person to clarify their intent. Notice the curiosity and request for more information (direct or implied). The hope is that the person shares more information that clarifies the message. Remember that tone of voice, inflection, and volume are also parts of communication. If someone says something sarcastically, it might imply that the content of their words is not trustworthy. So we can also ask for clarification by observing the incongruence of the tone or the affect: "I heard you say _____, but your tone (or body language) might indicate that you don't really feel that way." This is another way of asking for clarification. For a person who is reasonably emotionally healthy and somewhat self-aware, this is an opportunity to clarify their message by filling in the gaps of missing information or clearing up distortions. For some, remaining vague or evasive is part of their intended message, so the "clarification" will probably not help much.

I have met several people over the years who, for whatever reason, are not good at reading social cues. They do not comprehend subtleties of nonverbal communication like tone, facial expressions, or other body language. In our radio analogy, such difficulties constitute a problem with the receiver. There are ways that such people may become better at asking for clarification, but they will probably always prefer more concrete and direct communication from others.

For most of us, difficulty in receiving a message is due to distortions in the transmission or in the receiver. When communication is partial or distorted, there is missing information, and our brains tend to supply what is missing with assumptions, guesses, or historical information. In short, when info is missing, we tend to make stuff up to fill in the gaps. Because of our humanity, insecurities, and struggles, what we make up rarely comes from our best selves. It is critical to ask for information because we might make mistaken assumptions about others' intended message that align with our own insecurities or assumptions.

Other people can imply a message in what they say or do, and the goal of clarification is to make the implicit explicit. We also must monitor our assumptions and realize that what we think we heard is not necessarily what the person intended. If I am fearful that others do not like me, then when I hear an incomplete message, I might fill in the missing information with my fear and assume that my worst fears are true. The plots of many wonderful sitcoms are built around this premise. One character knows just enough information to assume that they know what is happening. They act as if it is true but then create difficulty when they interrupt or thwart a plan that has nothing to with the assumed behavior. Sadly, when this happens in real life it is not always funny. People can easily get their feelings hurt, and then the alligator brain kicks in because we can't distinguish between physical and emotional pain. We act out of the pain we feel, assuming intent on the other person's part, and may react or respond in a way that is disproportional to the situation.

We will talk more about conflict and misunderstandings in the next chapter, but for now I will say that remaining curious about ourselves and others and being open to the fact that we could be wrong in our assumptions is the beginning of a good, clarifying conversation. In one episode of the Apple TV+ show *Ted Lasso*, Ted's friends have gathered to listen to him share about a concern he has. The friends refer to themselves during such gatherings as the "Diamond Dogs." In this meeting of the Diamond Dogs, one of the friends offers Ted advice about his situation: "Find out before you freak out." He is encouraging Ted to see that he is making a series of assumptions about limited information and fretting about the possible eventualities. Ted needs to slow down, recognize that he is making assumptions, and "find out before he freaks out." Emotional health in such situations leads us to interrupt the alligator brain reaction, recognize the gap in information that we have filled with our own story, be curious about our feelings, and ask for the clarification we need.

I Focus

This recognition of how we contribute to communication distortion and the willingness to ask for clarification are part of what I call "I focus." If you have ever been to a workshop on communication or participated in relationship counseling, you have likely been encouraged to use "I statements" when communicating. This is in contrast to a "you statement." Instead of saying, "You don't listen to me," you might say, "I don't feel heard." The use of "you statements" often means you assign motivation to the other person that may be a distortion resulting from a story you have made up in the absence of full information. Using a "you statement" usually elicits a defensive response from the other person, who may want to argue about your perception of them. However, "I don't feel heard" is a factual statement about your own experience that does not assign a deficiency to the other person. Therefore, the other person is more likely to be able to hear your statement without a defensive reaction. (Note I said "more likely" and not "guaranteed.") Using "I statements" effectively and consistently requires intentionality and practice. They are awkward at first but become almost second nature the more they are practiced. Recognize that this is more than simply replacing "you" with "I." It is a shift to a new way of thinking.

I refer to this shift in thinking as "I focus." It begins by recognizing that the only thing that I can know for sure is my own experience, my own thoughts, and my own feelings. Though I might have a good guess about what another person means, feels, or thinks, I have to be aware that I cannot know this with 100 percent accuracy without a conversation (and maybe not even then). Then must come the awareness that I only have control over my own reactions, responses, and behaviors. This works best when we are more accurate in understanding our internal experience, thoughts, feelings, etc., but it is a good practice even when our internal dialogue contains partial or deleted information. The report of our own experience and seeking to frame our communication with others within that experience often leads to a better conversation. Such conversations help us and others grow in self-awareness. Cultivating awareness also benefits us in making us more patient and increasing our sense of empowerment.

As an example, suppose you meet regularly for lunch with a friend. You have to leave work for a limited lunch break, but your friend does not have such time constraints. When you meet with them, they are consistently late. Many people would never address the friend's tardiness. This avoidance might be motivated by a few different things, but it could be to avoid the conflict of a confrontation, believing that conflict might create a rift that could not be healed or, at a minimum, would be unpleasant. However, the friend's consistent tardiness might start to create a sense of resentment. Depending on your personality and experience, you might begin to think, "My friend knows my time from work is limited. They are consistently late. So they must not value their time with me, or maybe they don't like me as much as they used to." Because you only know that the friend is late and you don't know why, you tell yourself a story and begin to assign meaning or motivation to the friend's tardiness: "They don't respect me" or "They don't like me anymore." If we believe our assumptions are facts, we will have less productive conversations with the friend.

An "I focus" response begins with the reflection that you feel some resentment and have begun to make up stories about your friend's delays. You could address it with your friend by saying, "I'm curious about the fact that you are regularly late to our lunch meetings, and I'm worried that you don't really want to be here or there's something wrong between us." A better approach goes this way: "I've noticed that every time we meet, you seem to be significantly late. I'm curious if this is not a good time or if there's something going on." Realizing that the story you told yourself may not be *the* story or the full story, try being curious about what might be going on. Note that in the example I used the word "every," but be aware that "every", "always," and "never" are powerful words. They are generally best avoided unless it is literally true that something happens every time, always, or never. Often when we use such words, they communicate our feelings and not a literal fact. The person we are trying to talk to may then start arguing about the literality of the word and miss the feeling we wish to communicate. If you find yourself arguing about whether or not something happens *every time* instead of addressing the underlying concern, you have gotten off course in the conversation.

Suppose your friend responds, "I know I'm late. I'm just so disorganized. I'm late everywhere I go." You may know if this is true, but it might be. Perhaps they are a chronically late person and being late for lunch with you is not something you should take personally. However, your friend may want to avoid talking about something concerning your relationship, or they may be unaware how their tardiness affects you. You might follow your initial curiosity by adding information: "I hear you saying you're late everywhere. I had started to worry that maybe you were late to our lunches because there was an issue with me that we need to talk about." Now your friend can clarify. They might say, "I'm so sorry you've worried about that. It really doesn't have anything to do with you. Thank you for letting me know how that feels. I'll work on being on time." But they might also say, "I'm so sorry. I hadn't attributed this to my being late, but there is something we probably need to talk about." If you remain open and curious, your friend can tell you what they have been feeling. If it is the former statement, your friend might have gained insight into how you process their tardiness. You could also add, "I understand you are a person who often runs late, but my time for these meetings is so limited and I enjoy my time with you so much, I want to have as much time as we can have together." Note the "I statements" and the expression of personal thoughts and feelings. You and your friend might also have a conversation about other possible times to meet that would be more convenient. Perhaps you could propose a time when you are not on a lunch break from work. This option would not limit you to whether your friend is on time.

Summary

Other aspects of emotional and relational health will surface in the following chapters, but the traits discussed in this chapter are foundational. Relationships take time. They don't need a regular schedule like psychotherapy, but they require intentionality. Direct, open, honest communication is vital to a healthy relationship with ourselves and with others. Direct communication means communicating directly with another person when it is safe to do so and avoiding talking about that person, except to gain needed perspective to address the original person directly. It also means saying plainly what needs to be said without hoping the other person will get the message or trying to avoid saying difficult things to keep the peace. Speaking plainly about things does not have to be mean or cruel. We must also remember that we cannot control how others react or respond. We can accomplish these things by limiting our "alligator brain reactions" through minding our internal world—our thoughts, feelings, motivations, and beliefs. We can also avoid making assumptions about others and assigning motivation or intent to them. Instead, we should remain curious with them as well as with ourselves. When we seek to show up with these traits, we become a person who is trustworthy, and we invite the other person to respond in a similar way because we create an atmosphere of safety. Being able to monitor and manage ourselves also means we can respond better when the other does not bring their best self to a conversation. In such situations, we are creating safety for ourselves. We will explore this further in the next chapter.

Chapter 6

Dealing with Conflict & Empathic Failures

Because we are never perfect in our self-understanding and self-regulation, we sometimes fail in our empathy for others. We react out of our "alligator brain," respond with unhealthy defenses, and do things that inadvertently hurt others. In close friendships, as in psychotherapy, conflict and empathic failures are inevitable. How we navigate these when they occur determines if a relationship grows or ends after a difficult event. The idea of empathic failure as a therapeutic concept comes from the Interpersonal Psychiatry theory of Harry Stack Sullivan.

In my limited knowledge of Sullivan's theory, one of the things I like is that, unlike other developmental theories, his does not purport that our emotional lives are fixed in the first few years of life. Rather, they are created in every moment of our lives. This idea is hopeful because it means healing and growth can continue to occur throughout life. I like to think I can continue to grow and change in my personal life and as a therapist. I also want to work to create an environment that assists my clients to do the same. My first goal in psychotherapy is to meet people where they are, enter into relationship with them, join them in the journey of their lives, and hopefully help co-create a new reality. There is nothing more meaningful and humbling than achieving this goal as therapist and client. However, part of Harry Stack Sullivan's theory is that the therapeutic process also involves the relationship recovering from the therapist's empathic failures.

As a therapist, I begin to get to know my client from the first contact we make. One of the professors in my marriage and family program said the goal for the first session is to "join like crazy." In that first session, I want to understand the client's situation and story as best I can. I want to learn why they are seeking help, why now, and why they chose me. I also want to help the client feel safe and understood. I will answer any question they ask about me. I try my best to communicate what I hear from the client and my understanding of what they share. I also want to be sure that the therapy I offer will fit the client's needs. If I believe I can help, I try to lay out a general plan for our work together and ensure that the client desires to continue. As we continue to meet, I learn more and more about the client's story, feelings, and thoughts.

A friend once described the work of a psychotherapist as reading twenty to twenty-five novels at the same time. Every day, you take five or six of them off the shelf and read a chapter or two. It takes a minute to get reoriented to the characters and story, but then you are drawn back into the pages of the narrative. I thought this was a great way to describe the therapist's experience. However, this means that despite our best efforts, we sometimes forget small details, or we might confuse one person's story with another. At times, we may presuppose a client feels one thing when they feel something else. Such lapses may feel like a failure to the client, who rightly wants to be seen, remembered, and understood. Clients are generally good at correcting us in such situations without much difficulty. A therapist running late, forgetting a session, or being gone for illness or vacation can also feel like a lapse in care for a client. These empathic failures on the part of the therapist can create small setbacks in the therapeutic process, but Sullivan suggests that the work to recover from such failures is an important part of the therapy process for client and therapist. When we begin to recover from empathic failures in therapy, we are better equipped to deal with them outside of therapy and to be more tolerant when they occur. If we pay attention to the underlying feelings, we can also potentially learn about our internal processing and why certain things are hurtful to us. Life is full of little disappointments, and the ability not to define a relationship by those moments seems critical to authentic happiness.

Some people fear that conflict is a sign of difficulty in relationships, but it can be quite the opposite. Deepening, meaningful relationships will experience misunderstandings and conflict. When one or both people in the relationship avoid conflict or potentially difficult subjects, their intimacy will be limited. There is no risk and no vulnerability in a relationship that remains in the "safe zone." Those who practice group psychotherapy understand that the early phase of group development contains a period referred to as "pseudo-community" when all the participants are "playing nice" and seeking to get along. As people become more invested in a relationship, they may find it important to talk about things that are meaningful and important to them, including what bothers or hurts them. They will take risks to talk about deeper topics and will then risk misunderstanding. Conflict is a part of significant relationships, which is why learning to deal with it well is critical.

A couple of years ago, I had surgery that caused me to miss at least one therapy session with my own therapist. When I met with my therapist the next time, he asked how I was doing, and I thought he was asking about my recovery from surgery. I began to tell him about it. However, he was asking a general question about how I had been, and he admitted that he did not remember what had happened to me or what I was recovering from. I reminded him that I had surgery. I have seen this therapist for a while, and we have a good working relationship. We had talked about my surgery before it happened. I felt hurt that he did not remember it. I did not say anything in that session, but I thought about it between our sessions, and when we met again I said I wanted to talk about it. I told him how I had felt hurt by his forgetting about my surgery, and I did not want to just go on with therapy and pretend it was okay. (I feared that this would fester into anger or resentment and adversely affect our future therapy.) I said that I felt good about our relationship, and if we were to continue to meet, I needed to talk to him about this. He could hear my disappointment and he apologized. We talked about tools I use in my own practice to try to avoid such situations with my clients, but I also admitted that such things do happen to me.

In the end, we worked through this and have continued to have a meaningful working relationship.

In my own therapy practice, there have been moments when my empathic failures were bigger than the client's ability to tolerate (usually rightfully so). From time to time, my emotional reactions or misjudgments as a therapist result in a huge lapse in empathy. I know I am not alone in this as a therapist. However, after the early years of training, these larger lapses in empathy have generally been rare. When they do occur, they often result in clients leaving therapy altogether. For me, this is one of the most difficult things to deal with as a therapist. When such things happen to some therapists, they tend to blame their clients for their "lack of readiness to enter therapy," and there are times when that can be true, but I think it is important to recognize that we sometimes mess up. I am not talking about the gross misuse of a client or horrible bending of therapeutic boundaries; I mean failing to connect with clients in a way that is meaningful or reacting to them in ways that are hurtful. Also, a client may be fully justified in leaving, especially if the failure is egregious or happens several times. These types of failures often occur when we as therapists fail to keep our emotions and relational "baggage" out of the session. Therapy is about the person in front of us and not about us. A good therapist must have gone through some process (like their own therapy or another self-reflective experience) to maximize their ability to avoid big empathic misses. When we struggle as therapists with a certain type of client, we might want to avoid taking on clients with those particular issues. We might also want to seek professional supervision to help us better understand what triggers our blind spots or emotional reactions.

As therapists, we should focus on the client and their growth and understanding. One thing therapists do that is often confusing or frustrating to some people is redirect conflict or empathic misses back to the client. For example, a client may tell their therapist that they felt angry in a previous session when the therapist made a particular comment. The therapist might respond, "Tell me more about what angered you." They may follow a line of questions to help the client better understand his or her internal world and why a particular event or comment was hurtful. While others may disagree, I think that if the therapist has indeed done or said something that resulted in the client feeling hurt, an apology is appropriate. A friend would probably not engage in such a conversation regularly, but versions of this conversation are appropriate from time to time.

In friendships, the reactions to empathic misses can be similar to those in therapeutic relationships. We can have smaller empathic misses with a friend, or we may say or do something that is so hurtful that a friend withdraws from spending time with us. It is important to remember that conflict is not a sign of a bad relationship but can be an important part of a relationship deepening. Whether large or small, relationships will not continue to be meaningful if such challenges are not dealt with. How others respond to us in conflict (or how we manage conflict) can also indicate emotional safety and whether we can invest in a deeper relationship.

Anatomy of Conflict & Empathic Failure

It is impossible to predict all the ways relationships are adversely affected by the words or actions of two people. We have looked at potential places for relational difficulty in the previous two chapters. When we do not communicate fully or accurately, there is an opportunity for misunderstanding. With any gap of information, we tend to fill in missing information with our insecurities and presuppositions. If we are not aware and intentional, we may respond to another person as if our assumptions, projections, and misunderstandings are factual. We might assume the other intends to insult or harm us when we are simply filling in missing information with our own ideas. Reacting badly to a misunderstanding can often trigger the other person to respond defensively, and they may do or say something that continues the downward spiral of trading insults and injuries.

Conflict can also occur around exposed differences of opinion. These can be smaller like someone's taste in music or books or major like political or religious beliefs. Too often, our cultural context and emotional immaturity cause us to conflate ideas and people. We identify ourselves as our ideas or think of others as being their ideas.

If I like rock music (and I do) and someone else believes rock music is noise or, worse, demonic, that can feel like more than just a difference of opinion; it can feel like an insult to me as a person. Similarly, if I find out a friend voted for a different candidate than I did in the last election, I might feel like I can no longer be friends with them because I assume something about their personhood. We *are* people, and we *have* thoughts and opinions. A thought that is different from mine should not feel like a threat to me as a person. Two people who care about one another and are committed to a good relationship can exchange ideas, acknowledge that they think differently, and continue to care about one another. Too often in our divided society, we hear people insulting others because of their beliefs or stances on certain issues. Once we equate an idea with a person and allow that to affect our view of their value, we have lost sight of them as human beings.

From time to time, for a variety of reasons, a person might say something that feels insensitive or might be well intended but misses the mark. A friend may try to offer encouragement and say something that is hurtful. A person may make a comment about themselves or someone they know and not realize their comment has an unintended implication for you or someone you love. A person may offer reflections or feedback about any number of things, and if we hear them through a lens of shame, we can feel hurt and/or prompted to respond defensively.

Finally, others may intentionally or unintentionally deny our autonomy and seek to manipulate or force us to conform to their expectations for us. Phrases like "Because we are friends . . ." or "If you are truly my friend . . ." might indicate that someone is attempting to leverage friendship for a particular outcome. Regardless of motive, it is usually selfish because it reflects a person's intent on getting their own way despite the effect on others. At times, it may be that someone who is insecure or anxious unconsciously attempts to control a situation in order to lower their own anxiety. However, the experience of the one being controlled will probably feel the same regardless of the intentions of the person seeking to control an outcome.

Whether or not a given exchange is hurtful depends on a number of issues related to both parties in a relationship. However, as noted in the previous chapter, we cannot control the words and actions of other people (despite how much we might like to). Paul writes in Romans 12:17-18, "Do not repay anyone evil for evil, but take thought for what is noble in the sight of all. If it is possible, so far as it depends on you, live peaceably with all." We cannot control whether someone insults us or is mean (intentionally or unintentionally), but we can make sure we do not respond in kind. We cannot make another be less selfish, but we can identify our own selfishness and learn how to respond to another person's selfishness appropriately. We cannot make another person communicate more clearly, but we can work to communicate as clearly as we can and seek clarification and details when others are not clear. We cannot make another person treat us fairly, but we can set boundaries around what we are willing and able to do. And we cannot make others behave the way we wish they would, but we can understand our own feelings and learn how to communicate and respond in better ways. In the remainder of the chapter, I will discuss general rules that make managing conflict, misunderstandings, and disappointment more productive.

When We Have Hurt Someone

Many people think of "confrontation" as an angry or hostile word. However, *Dictionary.com* offers several uses of the word "confront" that include "to face and deal with boldly or directly" and "to bring together for examination or comparison" (2023). Direct conversation is not inherently hostile but can feel that way to someone who prefers ambiguity or wants to avoid conflict altogether. It can also be uncomfortable if someone brings up something we have said or done that has hurt them because it can trigger our shame or guilt about something we do not want exposed or examined. How we respond to such conversations with another person (a friend, a partner, a coworker, etc.) can have a huge impact on whether the relationship grows or withers. How we respond to another is often affected by *how* the person presents information to us. So it requires great awareness and intentionality to avoid responding in kind to another person who confronts us in an aggressive or hurtful way.

When someone says or does something hurtful, the passage from Romans above reminds us, "Don't repay anyone evil for evil." Evil may be a strong label for most of the interactions I might imagine, but if we are to change the tone of a conversation, we must be careful not to assume ill intent (until it is proven). We must remain open in order to hear what is being communicated (and not just what is being said), and we must seek to control our own "alligator brain" defenses. Just because something another person says hurts us does not mean that was their intent. What they said may be objectively hurtful, or we may experience it as hurtful due to our own sensitivities and insecurities. Remaining open and curious about the other's words and our reactions can be challenging, especially if what the other person says does not come from their best self and is offered in a harsh manner.

If a person approaches you from a place of being hurt or feeling hurt, they may not communicate well, and you need intentionality and patience to help clarify the message. Regardless of how well the message is communicated, the first step in receiving feedback is always the same: listen. Use active listening skills, including listening to the words and observing the tone and body language. Ask for clarification using the techniques and questions outlined in previous chapters. Focus on the other person's experience without initially offering any defense or feedback of your own.

In his book *Listening and Caring Skills*, John Savage describes a concept he borrowed from another person called "Fogging" (57). In this context, fogging refers to becoming like a fogbank that offers no resistance to anything that collides with it. The way Savage describes this, it is a non-defensive way of responding to another person that acknowledges whatever is true, true for you, or potentially true without offering any defense or explanation. He is clear that this is not *the* response but is a good start because it expresses openness without accepting everything that is said.

In chapter 5, I used an example of a friend who is regularly late for lunch. Imagine being that friend, and when you arrive at lunch on a particular day, the friend waiting for you says, "Well, it seems clear that you don't care about me or our relationship anymore. You are *never* on time, and it is so disrespectful to me. You obviously just don't care." That would be a lot to unpack, but let's try. The first thing you might observe is that your friend has an angry tone. However, if you understand that anger can cover hurt or threat, you might suspect that your friend feels something deeper than the anger they express. Your friend has at least dealt with your repeated lateness. What they say may or may not be an objective reality. What you can surmise is that it reflects how your friend feels. They feel that you are late every time, which seems to confirm their presupposition about your motive. If this type of outburst from your friend is atypical, you might want to know why it is coming up today. Maybe this is not about you, but they are having a difficult day, and they feel safe venting to you about your tardiness. There may be truth to the complaint, but the intensity of the reaction might be influenced by something else going on in your friend's life.

A good place to begin talking to this friend is by acknowledging their feelings and look how you might acknowledge anything potentially true for you. If you get bogged down in a conversation about how you don't appreciate their tone or whether or not you are *always* late, the conversation will likely be unproductive. You will not gain insight into yourself or be able to heal the hurt your friend is experiencing. You might start by saying, "Wow, you have strong feelings about this. Tell me more about what you are feeling" (asking for more information). Then you might say, "You're right that I'm late too often" (acknowledging the truth but not arguing how often it happens), and "I didn't realize how much this hurt your feelings" (stating a fact). The conversation could then unfold a number of ways as highlighted in the previous chapter. It is essential to maintain an open mindset, an open posture, and a good dose of humility. If you can admit that you have been late more times than you would like, you might need to reflect on why. Do you feel some resistance to meeting this person for lunch? Is there a problem with the meeting time, or is there indeed something about the person that has gone unaddressed? Is tardiness a general problem for you? Are you often late to most things in your life? You might need to tell the friend that you are not aware of any negative feelings about them, or you may have to admit that you are often late for a reason you need to talk about, but either way, you may owe them an apology.

A Good Apology

An apology is an important component of healing in a relationship when we have hurt someone else. It may be true that the other person has also hurt us, but pointing that out after they are honest about their pain is a defensive strategy of diversion. By putting the focus back on the other person and their behavior, we divert the attention from ourselves and our own actions. You may want to talk about the other person's behavior, but that will be more productive if you begin by taking responsibility for your actions. A good apology requires a healthy dose of non-reactive, non-anxious humility. We will explore how to manage our reactions and defenses in the next section. For now, even if you are able to keep from reacting or if you return to a person after a period of cooling down, you must still admit when you have been less than your ideal self.

A good apology is not saying a generic "I'm sorry." You might feel bad about what you did or feel bad that the other person is hurting, but "I'm sorry" does not express your understanding of what was hurtful. A good first apology is not saying, "I'm sorry you feel that way." But if you have spoken carefully and intentionally about another person's behavior and been truthful about what has hurt you, the other person may still respond with tears or anger. This reaction is a different defense that intentionally or unintentionally (or semi-intentionally) is intended to make you retract what you have said. In such a situation, you might say, "I understand you're angry, and I'm sorry that my bringing this up has hurt you; however, it's very important to me, and I believe we need to deal with it." In such a case, you acknowledge that you brought up something hurtful or angering without giving up the importance of the issue. When and how you present such matters to the other person is of critical importance.

Aside from that nuanced situation, a good apology acknowledges the specific hurtful behavior and acknowledges the other person's feelings. It also includes an element of true repentance. "Repentance" is a word often used in religions, and it means turning to a new way of thinking or being. It is not just feeling bad about something we have done. Simply feeling bad might reinforce feelings of shame. Only by acknowledging our behavior honestly can we begin to deal with it. Debilitating shame that prevents us from owning our own behavior inhibits change and increases the likelihood of repeating an unwanted behavior. At a minimum, true repentance means proposing how things will be different, not just promising generically that things will be different. Too often people feel bad about something they have done but want to avoid talking about it and instead say, "I'm sorry. It will never happen again." They expect the issue to be settled. In the example of being late to lunch, a good apology might sound like this: "I'm sorry I've been late so many times and that this has hurt you. I know your time for lunch is limited. The reality is that this time is not good for me. I've continued to try to make it work but obviously not successfully. I appreciate our time together. I wonder if we might find another time that might work for us both. I should have said something earlier. I'm truly sorry."

A more difficult conversation might be required when we have avoided dealing with something and are unconsciously late to keep from addressing it. In that case, we might say, "I'm sorry I've been late, and I hate that this has hurt you. The truth is that I felt hurt by something you said when we met several times ago, and I didn't talk to you about it then. I think that unconsciously I might be late because I'm avoiding the subject. We should probably talk about it if you are open to that." Notice that this is very different than a diversion technique. We are not saying, "Well, you're late too," or "Well, you hurt my feelings when we met a couple of months ago." This apology includes taking responsibility for our unintentional passive aggressive behavior/avoidance and invites a conversation about the underlying issue. It is not an attempt to avoid responsibility for our actions.

Finally, we must understand that if we have truly behaved in a hurtful way or said something hurtful, an apology does not magically erase the effects on the relationship. Too often we talk about "forgive and forget," but the reality is that our brains hold experiential memory and cognitive memory in different ways. We can choose to forgive with our cognitive mind, but the feeling of mistrust or hurt can linger. A relationship that has experienced hurt must be repaired by ongoing positive interaction. The other person needs to see that we are trying to follow through on our plans to work on the relationship. The other person might feel insecure for a while. We should be patient with them. If we say, "Good grief, are you still going on about that? I said I was sorry. Can't we move on?" we are discounting or dismissing the other person's feelings. We are also discounting our responsibility and minimizing our behavior. If the relationship continues to grow and heal, eventually the issue will become minimal or nonexistent, but we cannot rush the process for the other person because we feel shame about our actions. For more significant breaks in a relationship, instead of focusing on our personal discomfort and shame, we might focus on being grateful that this person is still a friend despite our empathic failure. We may learn about ourselves in the experience of grace, and we may be able to affirm something in the other person by taking their feelings and experience seriously.

Forgiveness

There is not sufficient space for a full examination of forgiveness in this book. However, it is important to note that biblical references to forgiveness almost exclusively concern times when we hurt another person. In the passage from the Sermon on the Mount in Matthew 5 referenced previously, Jesus encourages us to recognize when we have hurt another person and go to make it right. Frederick Keene provides a compelling look at the biblical language and historical context of passages on forgiveness in the New Testament (2010) and suggests that forgiveness is only possible between those who are cultural equals or when it is initiated by the party that holds power in a relationship. Because of this, we cannot demand forgiveness from another person, and that is why the repentance piece of an apology is critical in such situations. Keene suggests that repentance must include a recognition of and relinquishment of any power differential in order for true forgiveness to occur. The repentant person must seek to identify a plan for how things will be different going forward. A request for forgiveness that cannot acknowledge the other person's hurt or accept responsibility for their pain with a plan for change does not accomplish true restoration of relationships. This is why an insistence on forgiveness or a complaint about how the hurt party is dealing with the ongoing effects of their hurt is hollow and ineffective.

If we have been abused or mistreated by a person who holds power or authority over us—a boss, teacher, parent, pastor, or therapist, for example—we are not obligated to forgive without the other's true repentance. In such cases, we might find a way to forgive for our own well-being, but that takes a great deal of work. Keene observes that in Jesus's prayer on the cross, he did not directly offer forgiveness for those who exercised power over him in order to kill him, but instead he prayed that God the Father, who retains all power, would forgive them. Sometimes, when we have been hurt, the best we can muster is a hope to want to forgive the person one day. In such times, we might be able to pray, "God, I'm not yet in a place where I can forgive this person who has hurt me, but I pray that you will." Implied in the prayer is hope that the other person will find true repentance, accept responsibility for their actions, and recognize their need to change.

When Our Alligator Brain Is Activated

Sometimes another person may bring up something or say or do something so hurtful that our reptilian defenses are activated, and we may respond poorly. As mentioned earlier, our brains do not differentiate between emotional and physical pain. When we feel hurt, our instinct may be to respond in kind and do something to try to hurt the other person (fight). We may feel overwhelmed by our emotions and want to leave either the immediate situation or the relationship altogether (flight). Finally, we may not be able to function and not know what to do (freeze). If you have ever left a tense situation with someone and then had a flood of emotion or thoughts of what you wish you had said, you might have experienced this state. These alligator responses of "fight," "flight," or "freeze" are instinctual responses of our autonomic nervous system, and regardless of how much we work on them, they can still get the better of us from time to time. Completely overcoming our acute stress responses is not a realistic goal. Learning to better control them and not allowing them to control us is a better goal. Progress, not perfection.

As I described previously, there is a brief moment between a stimulus and an alligator response in which we can interrupt this reaction. When we first start working on it, simply having the awareness that the response has occurred is progress. We may be triggered by something a person says or does and respond poorly, only to realize that we were affected in that way. The next step is to start trying to identify what prompted the reptilian response. We may have reacted with anger or simply retreated from a situation. Once we realize that we have reacted in this fight or flight manner, we can begin to reflect on our underlying feelings. If anger is often a secondary emotion, which ones are primary? We might have felt hurt by something said or done, or we might have felt threatened. A threat might register with us as "fear." We might be afraid of a particular outcome or what the person's words or actions mean. In our fear, we might respond with anger instead of dealing with the underlying threat or feeling of fear. A threat may also be implied or a product of our own interpretation.

At various times in my early married life, when we were struggling financially, I sometimes got angry with bill collectors who contacted me about late payments. I realized over time that I experienced a threat in those calls, but it was a threat to my idealized self-image. Not being able to provide for my family and not having sufficient money to pay all our bills on time led me to feel inadequate. To my unconscious brain, the bill collector calling was a reminder of my perceived failure. I responded in anger at them, but I was disappointed and angry with myself. Identifying the underlying hurt or threat is not always simple or direct and may require help through talking with another friend or a professional.

Sometimes when we feel emotionally flooded, we want to leave. Sometimes leaving is a good way to avoid saying or doing something retaliatory in response to another person. "The rules of engagement," as I might call them, allow for a break to cool down and collect our thoughts, but leaving can prompt the other person to feel abandoned or confused. So the mindful response might be to claim the need for space and say something like, "I'm feeling a bit overwhelmed. I'm going to go (for a walk or to the gym, etc.), and I'll talk to you later." The last part is important. If you call time out in an argument or discussion, you need to be the one who calls time in. The affirmation of return is critical. I included the "walk" or "the gym" because exercise can be a good way to turn emotional energy into kinetic energy and help organize your thoughts and feelings. Whatever you do to calm yourself and collect your thoughts, when you have had a chance to cool down, it is time to reengage.

Ultimately, the goal is to have an awareness of feelings and internal self-analysis occur in the moment the response is activated. This can happen with practice, and it works best when you try to slow down your responses. Don't immediately do what you impulsively feel like doing. Evaluate your feelings and ask yourself what you are feeling and why. The "why" may be important. You may feel angry, sad, or threatened (afraid) because you have added meaning or motivation to what you experienced or heard. A friend or partner may say something that you think can only mean one thing, and you know what that is. Except you may be wrong. You might be 99.9 percent sure you are right, but that 0.1 percent is enough to slow down. Instead of responding with your alligator anger, you might say, "When you said that, what I heard was _____ ,and I felt angry" (or better yet ". . . and that scared me or hurt me"). At this point, you will likely have a better conversation. You will hopefully get clarity about a person's intentions and can adjust your response accordingly. Remember the encouragement from *Ted Lasso*: "find out before you freak out."

Again, there is no such thing as perfection in mastering the alligator brain. I tell people that I talk about our acute response regularly and teach about it for a living. I have so many years of personal therapy that I have lost count of the number. I have gotten pretty good at interrupting the alligator response and having better conversations, but under stress, when I am tired, when I am preoccupied, and the like, that alligator response is right there, ready to get the better of me. When it happens, I am generally good at recognizing it and coming back with a better response and an apology. However, I am never perfect, and, again, perfection is not the goal.

When Someone Has Hurt Us

Remember the admonishment about worship in Matthew 5:13: if you are making a gift at the altar and realize that your brother or sister has something against you, leave your gift, and go be reconciled with that person (paraphrase). When we hurt another person, we need to take responsibility to make it right with them. However, if someone hurts us or we hold something against another person, how do we handle that? Paul's words in Romans 12 remind us that we have a responsibility to try to make things right with others, but we are not responsible for their reaction or their willingness to engage with us. We can only "clean our side of the street." To do this, we must be honest with ourselves about our own feelings, words, and actions. We have to maintain a sense of humility about our thoughts and assumptions and make sure we address our concerns with the other person in a way that maximizes their opportunity to hear us. We should try to speak in a way that is least likely to evoke a defensive response. Let us remember that we will not be perfect at this, and we ultimately cannot control the other person's response or reaction.

The first step in addressing someone's complaints when we have hurt them is to use active listening skills and ask clarifying questions. The first step in addressing being hurt by another person is also to listen—but to listen to ourselves. We need to identify the underlying issues and feelings. We need to evaluate how we contributed to the situation. We need to evaluate whether we are making a potential assumption about the other person's words or behavior that colors our perception of events. When our emotions are high or when we are in our "alligator brains," it can be difficult to reflect on these points. It is often easier to focus on a singular interpretation and perspective and then react to that. In such cases, a temporary relational triangle might be helpful. Talking to another friend or a therapist can help us get clarity about our own actions, reactions, thoughts, and feelings.

Once we identify the underlying feelings, we may want to try to discern whether they are based on objective facts or on an interpretation of the events/words that we have added. Again, a third party might be able to help us with this. If we need information to address this, we might begin a conversation with a friend: "When you did (or said) _____, I was confused by what you meant. I was afraid it might mean _____." Notice this does not start with an accusation but with a desire for more information. It also involves recognizing our initial feelings but being willing to postpone our reaction until we have more information. We strive not to assume the veracity of our own interpretation. Whether we have a conversation like this or are not yet ready to engage with our friend, at least one other step needs to occur: evaluate any potential way we might have contributed to the difficulty.

In a particular event, we may need to be aware of certain things and take responsibility for how we contributed to the situation. For example, several years ago, I was preaching at a big church in the Nashville area. I left my house later than I intended to get to the church that morning and was driving a bit faster than the speed limit. I came up behind someone driving less than the posted speed limit, and I could not get around them to pass. I grew impatient and frustrated with the driver. In that moment, I did not behave in a way that expressed my anger (although I have not been perfect at that in my life either). However, in that moment, I realized that if I had not left my house late and had given myself enough time to get to the church on time, I would probably not feel so impatient and angry. This helped me relax a little. The other driver was not the problem; it was my own lack of organization and preparedness that morning.

Similarly, I had several recent conversations that involved scenarios like the following composite story:

> I have been irritable all week. I have been very busy with my own work and taking care of things related to [a recent crisis in my life], but so many people were asking things of me, and I had to

take care of those things. I have been angry with these people who know I am dealing with this [recent crisis] and am trying to just manage my life, but they keep giving me more and more to do. It is overwhelming and I am sick of it.

I have felt this way in the past and thought that others were being "so insensitive" to my needs. However, the underlying assumption in this story is that we have to say yes when asked to do things. Of course, that is sometimes true, especially when related to work or other obligations to which we have committed. But just because we *can* do something does not mean we *must* do something. We often say yes to things we are asked to do out of fear of disappointing others. We may even feel like there is no one else who can do a particular thing, so we are obligated to do it. I have come to realize that others are rarely malicious in their intent. If we are good at certain things, we will be asked to do them again and again. Others will ask things of us but generally expect us to be able to say no if we need to. People are not usually thinking, "Oh, you're doing too much. I'm not going to ask you do such and such." Instead, they think, "Chris is so good at doing such and such, and we need someone to do that. I will ask him and see if he is able." We may not want to disappoint others, or we may like doing certain things. The problem is not that others ask; the problem is that we say yes. This is part of the "I focus" that I think is so important in relationships. We have to recognize when the problem is our expectations, our inability to say no, or our struggle to recognize another person's (or our own) autonomy.

Similarly, we may feel frustrated that someone did not do something we asked them to do. But humility and that 0.1 percent chance we might be wrong should open us to the possibility that we did not ask, did not ask clearly, or did not indicate the importance of the task to the other person. Instead of expressing anger at someone for not doing what we ask, we might use the "I statements" and the "I focus" and begin the conversation like this: "I wanted to talk to you about [that event]. I'm afraid I may not have been clear about what I wanted/needed." We could also begin with our own feelings: "I was disappointed that you did not _____. However, I realize I may not have been clear about how important that was to me." The other person may then offer an apology or explanation. We may learn that we indeed did not make our wishes clear. However, the other person might say they did understand but were not able to fulfill the request for a reason we don't know about. Taking responsibility for how we might have contributed to the problem we want to discuss is one aspect of the "I focus" that can help soften a potential conflict.

Once we discover our true underlying feelings, sort out ways that we may have contributed to the situation, and are in a place of relative emotional stability, it might be time to address our concerns with a friend. We need to find the right time and space, and we don't need to sort out the conflict out unilaterally. We might say, "I would like to talk with you about something. When would be a good time to visit?" We should find a place to meet that is appropriate. If we are likely to feel strong emotions or fear that our friend might, we might find a place that is more private than a public place. (However, if we fear a strong negative reaction, meeting in a public place might keep our friend from overreacting and provide a bit of safety.) When we do finally meet, some ways to talk about our concerns are better than others.

First, we should focus on objective and observable facts. If we veer into feelings or conjecture, let's do so with humility. We might be able to say, "It seems to me that since X happened, you have felt angry." In this statement, we are talking about our perception. It has the "I focus" because it states our perception but is not an accusation. We are not saying, "Since X has happened, you have been so angry." While the interpretation of anger might be accurate, stating it without acknowledging it is our perspective sounds more like an accusation and may elicit a defensive response. Phrases that reflect "what I have seen" or "I have felt" are more about our experience. In the scenario with the friend late to lunch, we might say, "It seems to me that you've been late every time" or "I think you've been late more times than not." The former is a perception; the latter is an attempt at an objective truth but contains the phrase "I think," an element of humility that acknowledges we could be wrong. Our friend might deny the latter but cannot deny the former, since it is a statement of our experience. That is nonnegotiable; it is *our* experience.

Second, avoid assigning any motivation or intention to the other person's behavior. It might feel like someone intends to hurt us, but that does not mean they do. Even if we have an educated guess about their intent, we could be wrong. Similarly, "I feel like" is not a statement of feeling; it is a statement of experience or perception. It might better be stated, "It seems to me" or "I am afraid that." Avoid the phrase "feels like" if it is a not-so-veiled attempt at an insult. "I feel like you are a jerk (or worse)" is technically an "I" statement; however, it reveals little about the person making the statement and is more an attempt at name calling or labeling the other person. If we are truly I-focused, the only thing we can know with certainty is our own thoughts, our own feelings, our own experiences, and what we see or hear with our senses. We should be aware that our own experience might be distorted by a number of different things discussed in earlier sections. We must also recognize that we cannot or should not speak for others. Another person's relationship with the person we are talking to is between the two of them. We might say we did not like the way the other person was treated, and we may have feelings about that, but we should not say the other person is upset about it or that "lots of people feel this way." We can only speak for ourselves and how we experience events or are affected by the other person's actions.

The focus of a conversation like this is much healthier if love for the friend is our priority and we intend to help solve the problem of the broken relationship. An attempt to hurt, control, embarrass, or elicit any other outcome ignores Paul's encouragement to focus on what is noble and seek peace as much as possible (Rom 12:17-18).

When Reconciliation May Not Be Possible (& When It Is)

As I mentioned earlier, sometimes our empathic failures are so big that we cannot mend them. At times, we may feel so hurt that we cannot bring ourselves to try to work on the relationship at the moment. Or maybe we have done our best to "clean our side of the street," but the other person is not ready to work on mending things. We cannot control other people. We can't make people understand us or feel what we wish they would feel. In such situations, we have to lean into the love for another person that allows them the autonomy or freedom to handle something their way. Remember that "love does not seek its own way (for the other person)" (see 1 Corinthians 13:5). This aspect of mature love can be difficult, especially for people pleasers. We want others to understand us. We want to work out our issues. We want to be able to make things better, but we cannot control how others deal with empathic failures in relationships. I will discuss more about when relationships end in the final chapter, but for now I will acknowledge that sometimes, for a variety of reasons, relationships are broken beyond repair. We can only work on our part; we can't force others to work on theirs. It is important to remain open to possible reconciliation and continue to work on ourselves. This makes us better for other current relationships and for future relationships, and it may increase the likelihood of repairing a broken relationship.

Several years ago, the executive director left the nonprofit where I worked. I was serving in a leadership position at the organization and made assumptions about what my role would be in the interim period after the director's exit. However, what I experienced felt like a struggle for power between at least two factions of employees. The result was a split in the organization. Without better conversations at the time, "my experience" was based on assumptions and interpretations that were not necessarily factual and certainly did not match others' experience. The initial experience of animus prompted some others to leave the organization, and I took their departure personally and felt hurt. But with time, I began to feel that the relationships experienced some healing, though they were not restored to previous levels of connection. In a conversation with a mutual friend, I learned that one of the people who left had lingering feelings about me that we had never talked about. I contacted this person offered to talk about it. We agreed to meet, and I listened as my friend described the split in the organization from her perspective. It was *her* experience, but it was not completely foreign to me. Enough time had passed, and I had continued to work on my own growth to the point that I could acknowledge who I was at that time in my life and the fears and insecurities that influenced my behavior. I had believed that my friend misunderstood the events, but I needed to admit that I was also guilty of misunderstanding. My friend experienced one of our conversations as my expression of strong anger. I did not recall the conversation as she did, but I could admit that I had misunderstood the fullness of situation, read into some things, and subsequently acted badly out of my own fear and insecurity. I apologized for the part I had played, and I expressed remorse that I had not known about these lingering feelings. Our relationship was not permanently broken, but it had changed. There was room for conversation and healing because the relationship remained important to both of us. I am glad to continue to call this person my friend.

Bears

Sometimes when reconciliation is not possible, keeping distance is the best option. There are times when we cannot avoid being around certain people, but we don't experience them as safe. Indeed, some people prove themselves to be unsafe again and again. In identifying such people, we must be careful not simply to label someone we don't like, does not agree with us, or does not behave as we wish. Truly unsafe people are identified that way in more than one part of their lives by more than one person because their way of relating to the world is less adaptive. Lindsay Gibson describes such people as "Emotionally Immature" in her book *Adult Children of Emotionally Immature Parents* (2015). Alan Godwin refers to them as "Drama People" in his book *How to Solve Your People Problems* (2008). Since a complete description is beyond the scope of this project, see these books for in-depth descriptions of unsafe, problematic people. I will, however, offer the analogy of "bears" to describe them.

For most people, to some extent, their reactions, behaviors, interactions, and responses are adapted to the context and the relationship in which those things occur. They have the ability to say things like, "What I wanted to say to her was x, but I realized it was not appropriate in that setting." The ability to observe yourself in each situation and make changes in how you interact, as much as possible, indicates some level of emotional adaptability and health. What I observe and experience in my encounters with unsafe people is that they react, respond, or interact in any situation in generally predictable and fixed ways. For example, a person who tends to be overly focused on himself immediately reacts to any news by saying something about himself and how the news will affect him. That same person might be focused on his own needs as others are clearly hurting or more significantly affected by the situation. Another example might be a person who is always suspicious of others and regularly assigns ill-intent to anything another person says. She might even twist a compliment into a criticism. You might say to her, "Your dress today is very pretty. I love it," and receive the response, "I guess you don't like the things I regularly wear." This fixed way of relating might be true about, but not limited to, people who regularly try to get their own way, who are highly critical, who are easily offended and angry, who are not able to talk about deep or difficult subjects, or who avoid difficult emotions.

Unfortunately, such people often carry a deep level of shame and do not choose to behave as they do. Just because their behavior might be unconscious doesn't mean it isn't hurtful. Such people lack insight into themselves and disavow direct confrontation of their behavior, often enacting one or more of the defenses listed in chapter 4 to blame others for their behavior or to justify or explain their behavior. For this reason, a conversation with them can often leave you questioning yourself rather than affirming your perspective. Encounters with such people are why we need to have reliable "mirrors" in our lives that help counter the distorted image of ourselves that they might reflect to us.

Because of these traits, I began to refer to such people as "bears." Bears always do what bears do. If you leave your food out when camping, a bear will eat your food. He does not care how hard it was for you to pack it in or how expensive it would be to replace it. If you get too close to a bear cub, the mama bear will maul you. She does not care about your intentions or whether you are actively hostile.

A bear does what a bear does. Because of this, we cannot reason with bears. They respond out of their instincts, and they perceive the world the way they perceive it. We cannot reason a bear out of their perspective or behavior.

The first time you go camping and leave your food out and the bear eats it, you might be angry with the bear. You might even, theoretically, try to reason with the bear about how they should not do that. The second time you leave your food out (because you believe the bear has learned a lesson), you might be angry at the bear "for not listening to you." But at some point, you have to accept that the bear is always going to do what a bear does. We don't change bears. For this reason, people do not leave their food where bears can get it. They put their food in lockers or hang it in trees. People who are around bears have to consider that the bears are potentially harmful, and they need to prepare.

To extend the analogy, a person might point out that bears can potentially be trained. Imagine we could train a bear to ride a tricycle. We might be able to keep a bear from behaving in an aggressive manner, and we may get him to do what we want him to do, but the bear will only comply with the programming he is given. He will not understand the value of riding a trike and will not go looking for a trike the next time he needs to go somewhere. We are not fundamentally changing the bear's nature, but we *might* be able to get him to approximate a desired behavior.

Such training for bears is accomplished by a series of rewards and consequences. It is not accomplished by giving the bear instructions on how to ride a tricycle and reasoning with the bear about the need to practice. Many people have pushed themselves to the point of exhaustion trying to reason with and change the bears in their lives. People wind up doing this because most people are adaptable. If someone we love said, "I wanted to let you know that when you did x, I felt hurt," we might have one of the conversations outlined earlier in the chapter, but we will evaluate the person's comments, observe the effect on the person we care about, and probably try to shift how we interact because we care about how we affect the other person and want to maintain a good relationship. Most people can adapt like this to some extent or another, so we think that if we simply explain ourselves well enough to the other person, something will change. For people who are more emotionally healthy, this is true. That's why we continue frustrating and exhausting ourselves trying to convince a bear that it shouldn't eat our food, metaphorically speaking.

For people prone to seek their own way in relationships, reading this section may cause them to think of someone they have talked to about a particular behavior again and again, and the person has not changed. They may not be open to reflecting on whether what they ask is reasonable. The other person's objections to being controlled may not register as reasonable. A person's unwillingness to comply with something we want them to do does not make them a "bear." Having someone we trust to talk to may help us figure out if we are reasonable in asking the person to change to accommodate our wishes. People don't have to change just because we want them to. We may be the ones who need to change. We may need to change our expectations of the other person.

Again, remember that "love does not seek its own way." If we continue to encounter a "bear" in our lives, instead of continuing to get frustrated trying to change the bear, we may need to allow the bear to be a bear. This will probably mean we have to learn how to avoid the bear or be careful about how we behave around the bear, but we won't continue to waste time and energy trying to change someone who does not want to change or continues to deny that there is a problem.

Summary

Some people in the world enjoy conflict, but most people do not. Conflict is never easy. However, there are times when conflict is a sign of a maturing and deepening relationship. Whether someone brings something to us that we need to talk about or we take something to someone else, the primary goal should be love and reconciliation. We cannot always control the latter, but we can always strive for the former. Conflict to solve a problem is different from conflict designed to hurt or control someone. We cannot control how others approach us or respond to us, but we can control how we initiate conversations and how we react to others. In moments when our defenses are activated and we do not respond out of our best selves, we can seek understanding, take responsibility, and apologize. How we manage ourselves in conflict is the most important factor in determining whether relationships deepen or wither. We cannot always find healing for a rift in a relationship, but we should seek to keep our "side of the street" clean.

Chapter 7

Support in a Crisis

We all can understand suffering in one way or another. As human beings, we are subject to the vulnerability of need that is not satisfied. As bodied creatures, we are subject to cold, hunger, injury, illness, and death. As reflective beings, we can be tortured by decisions we have made with unintended consequences and the "what if" of the road(s) not taken. As emotional beings, we are subject to sadness, loneliness, depression, and regret.

I am grateful for my high school English teacher, Dr. Offutt, for introducing me to the literature and concepts of existentialism. We experience suffering when we make choices to protect ourselves while others suffer, or we choose to sacrifice ourselves to ease another's suffering. Each decision involves one or more option(s) that is not taken. Ultimately, our lives become the result of our collective decisions, and we must live with the existential reality of the joys and sorrows resulting from each choice (conscious or unconscious) we have made.

We are also subject to being hurt by other people's intentional and unintentional decisions and actions. Buddhist belief begins with the concept of life as suffering. In many ways, this is true. Ultimately, suffering helps us make meaning and define ourselves. We tend to try to avoid things that can hurt us or potentially hurt us. Regardless of the nature of our suffering, many people learn ways to cope so that not all suffering is a "crisis." Having someone present with us in suffering as outlined in earlier chapters is a critical part of coping, but sometimes our suffering reaches a crisis level.

While we can clearly identify some experiences of suffering as crises—a natural disaster, the loss of a loved one, an accident, illness, or the loss of a job—the idea can also be subjective. To an adult, a teenager's crisis may not seem significant. What feels like a crisis to one person may not seem like one to another. It may be that a crisis occurs any time a person's current circumstances overwhelm their usual coping mechanisms. Most of us have ways to deal with the stress of daily life. Some ways may be healthier than others, but whatever it is, it works. However, there are times in life when we experience a tragic event that overwhelms our ability to cope for a while. There are also times when we might experience a series of smaller challenges in a relatively short period, and the cumulative effect is overwhelming. Imagine waves in the ocean. You can experience one huge, devastating tsunami, or you might get hit by a bigger than average wave that knocks you down, and before you get your feet under your, you are hit by another and maybe another. In either situation, it can be hard to find your bearings again and move forward. Many people seek counseling in times like these. Most counselors, but not all, are well trained in helping people learn to face such situations.

If a distraught person has not experienced a tsunami-type tragedy, they may not even realize they are in a state of crisis. Or a person might feel like they are in a crisis but not know why. Therapists should be able to help clients identify and evaluate the crisis they are experiencing. Understanding what has changed or what has happened to create the current circumstance can often help explain the client's response and reveal ways they might recover. At times, the cause is clear, like when someone has lost their job and worries how they will survive. Other times a crisis may relate more to how a person interprets a particular event. When I worked as a hospital chaplain, I was visiting a patient and his wife after the patient was admitted. They were waiting for test results. I happened to be in the room when the doctor arrived to share the results. The couple asked me to stay, and I did. When the doctor told them what he had found, both the patient and his wife had immediate strong, emotional reactions. The wife broke down in tears, and the man was obviously terrified. The doctor continued to describe the proposed treatment, and while it would not be easy, he was optimistic about recovery. After the doctor left, I asked the couple what they were feeling. The wife described how they recently had a friend with the same diagnosis who had died from the condition. So when the doctor told them the husband had this diagnosis, they heard it as a death sentence. This couple had difficulty finding hope in the situation because of their previous experience. The words about treatment and the possibility of recovery had not registered with them or comforted them. Their earlier experiences shaped how they heard the news, and while the news itself was not good, their fears amplified it. At times, these underlying interpretations might occur more at an unconscious level, and it might require several conversations to finally uncover what drives the overwhelming response.

I saw a couple in psychotherapy who continued to have arguments about a variety of issues. Their arguments had pushed them to the point of crisis, and one of them introduced the possibility of divorce. We met for several sessions, and one day, they talked about a fight they had regarding shelving in a closet. (Yes, shelving. So I was pretty sure something bigger was going on.) In the heat of their exchange, the man blurted out, "I don't want her to control me like my mother did." With further exploration, we began to understand that he was on guard in every conversation because he feared losing his autonomy. With additional work, they were able to work through this and lower the overall level of conflict in their relationship.

For many people in a crisis, maybe even most, there is no need to explore the possible unconscious factors but just a need for someone to help them understand their situation, explore their options, and figure out a realistic plan to move forward. A friend can provide this support in a crisis if they are attuned to listening and can avoid the potential pitfalls and missteps. Again, there is no way to cover every type of crisis or tragedy in the space of this chapter. However, I would like to share general guidelines for what is helpful and unhelpful in trying to offer support to a friend in need.

Be Present, Listen, & Clarify

One of the seminal beliefs of Christianity is that Jesus is the incarnate presence of God on earth, "Immanuel" or "God with us." People of other religious faiths tend to shun the idea of a god who takes human form and reject the idea that a human can be God. But the Christian belief that God loved us enough to take on our form and experience life as we do means we are in relationship with a God who understands what it is to be physically hurt, relationally betrayed, emotionally sad, or spiritually tempted. For us, Jesus is not half human and half God but is both fully human and fully God. Part of God's care for involves seeking to understands our earthly existence experientially. When we seek to understand another person and empathize with their situation—to truly understand their situation from their perspective—we live by Christ's example and love as God has loved us. In being present with others, we seek to embody the love of God for them in the same way God loved us through Jesus, the embodiment of God with us.

Many verses from the Bible directly or indirectly apply to being present and listening. In Romans 12, Paul writes, "Rejoice with those who rejoice; weep with those who weep" (v. 15). This is an encouragement to cultivate empathy. It also implies that we must be intentional about how we are present with others. Being able to rejoice with others seems easy, but if a person rejoices over good fortune and we feel envious, rejoicing with them might be difficult for us. We must set aside our own feelings—not discount or suppress them but momentarily set them aside—to be able to be present with another person's feelings of joy. At a minimum, we need to be aware of our feelings in the moment.

Over the years, we have had times of financial struggle: when I was in my training programs, when my wife or I lost jobs, or when we had big losses or unexpected expenses. Sometimes we have worried about paying for the necessities of life. In some of those times, I was able to visit with friends at church or other parts of my life who were having the opposite experience and celebrating promotions, new cars, or new houses. It was difficult at times to set my envy aside to celebrate with my friends, but I have read and heard that "love is not envious" (1 Cor 13:4). When I read that and heard it at many weddings, it was part of a long list of things that seemed obvious and didn't seem that ominous, but loving in this way is challenging.

On the other hand, our ability to "weep with those who weep" (Rom 12:15) is directly affected by our general feelings about sadness and our personal comfort with crying. In some instances, when another person is sad, we feel uncomfortable and try to say something to make it better, or we try to encourage them to stop crying. In some terrible reactions, a parent might even try to force a child to stop crying by saying, "Stop crying or I will give you something to cry about." In all of this, the attempt is often to ease or change the other person's feelings because of our own discomfort with their emotions. It is a true gift to be present with someone who is sad and crying and allow ourselves to be so present and connected to their situation that we also feel sad or cry. Being present with another person means setting aside our own thoughts and feelings momentarily in order to hear and understand their feelings. It means allowing ourselves to be uncomfortable without having to try to "fix it." Remember that "love does not seek its own way" (1 Cor 13:5).

By this point in the book, you know that the first step in almost any situation is to listen. When a friend is overwhelmed or experiencing a tragedy, listening is critical. To listen, we have to be present both physically and emotionally. Being as emotionally available as possible is important. Our physical presence might be through a phone call or an in-person visit depending on the situation. If you are at work and a friend comes to you or calls you and says, "I'm having a difficult time right now and I need to talk to someone about it," what happens next depends on a lot of things. I have known people who would immediately drop what they were doing and neglect their own plans in order to listen to their friend. Then, when they cannot meet their own obligations, they excuse it by saying they "*had* to help a friend." In this case, helping a friend in a crisis creates a crisis for the person trying to offer help. However, depending on the issue, this may not be acceptable or necessary. In most circumstances, it is reasonable to examine your own needs when offering help to another person. You might have a meeting in twenty minutes and not be able to offer much at the moment. So you might say to your friend in need, "I only have about twenty minutes to talk right now. I don't know if that's enough for what you need to talk about. If not, why don't we see if we can find time later over lunch or after work?"

If we are the one in crisis, we might want to be aware of our needs and the other person's when we seek help. We should be proactive in asking for help when we need it. This positive sign indicates strength. But if we just call a friend and go into their office with whatever is bothering us without regard for their time, we might be disappointed and not get what we need in the moment. We might say, "Hey, I'm having a difficult time today. I'd like to talk to someone. Do you have time to talk now?" This puts us in a better position to get the time we need for what we want.

Once you set aside a time to meet, make sure you meet in a place suitable for what you need to talk about. If you anticipate strong emotions about something, suggest talking in a less public place. Once you have a place and time, prepare to listen and be emotionally present.

All the active listening skills from chapter 3—including being a non-anxious, active listener and asking good, clarifying questions—are critical in these circumstances, but keep certain goals in mind when you seek to help a friend in crisis. A person who is experiencing a big life event will likely want to tell you the story of what has happened. Memory of tragic events (and memory in general) is not static. How we remember events is often affected by a number of factors, including how we feel. Also, each time we access a memory, we do so from a point in the future when more information might be available or when our circumstances have changed, and the new experience and knowledge might affect what we remember. People are also more likely to remember events in a way that is most acceptable to their own ego strength. This means we tend to forget details that do not fit with our ideal image of ourselves (or others) and remember events in a way that offers a plausible explanation for our own feelings, experiences, and behaviors. Early in a crisis, things may feel chaotic with many details or pieces of information. This is the time when talking to a caring, non-anxious listener is critical to bringing order to the chaos. That conversation begins to lay the foundation of meaning that a person will eventually make of their situation. As a person learns or understands more, their narrative of what has happened might reflect the new information.

When you first meet with someone experiencing a crisis, they may announce the headline first, like "My wife is leaving me," "My dad died," or "I got fired." You might simply offer emotional support that patiently invites the rest of the story: "Oh my gosh, I am so sorry. What happened?" Allow the other person to tell you what they want or need to tell you. Remember that telling this story is important for them, so try not to interrupt more than necessary. Ask clarifying questions that will help you understand the situation. Ask how the person is feeling, remembering that they may not know yet. They may feel only "numb" or "in shock" depending on the event. Also remember that what they feel may not be what you would feel or what you expect, so stay curious and receptive to whatever the other person may share.

Countertransference & Shared Trauma

I mentioned this subject in chapter 3 and will add more here. Depending on what a person shares with you or what happened to them, their story may connect to something in your life that stirs strong feelings. The listener's internal reaction to what someone shares is clinically referred to as "countertransference." ("Transference" is the sharing person's unconscious experience of the listening person.) Sorting out which feelings are based on your personal experience and which are communicated by the other person can be critical in being a comforting and empathetic presence. Even if the person's experience is not something you have gone through, hearing the story may still trigger strong emotions for you. Allowing yourself to be open to another person's pain and story can evoke strong emotions and might even overwhelm you at times. This is one reason that the encouragement to "weep with those who weep" is not to be taken lightly. Strong feelings and reactions stirred by hearing another person's story are sometimes referred to as vicarious trauma. Remember that not all crises are traumatic, but the experience of hearing someone's story can have a vicarious emotional impact.

Some people work in positions where they experience such stories on a regular basis: first responders, chaplains, therapists, and clergy. For them, the repetitive exposure to vicarious trauma or emotional experience can have a cumulative effect of burnout over time without proper care. We all benefit from self-care activities so that we can be more present with others. These include any activity that connects you to body, mind, and spirit. Yoga, other kinds of exercise, hiking, meditation, prayer, quality time with a friend or group of friends, gardening, or caring for pets are good examples. Another part of self-care involves connecting with our inner world. Participating in a process of psychotherapy or related work can help us discover our internal motivations and identify our feelings. Understanding how we feel and what we think, and making space for that within ourselves, can help us feel less anxious, more grounded, and better able to connect with God and others.

A Plan for Help in a Crisis

When a person finishes telling you what happened to them and when you feel like you understand the situation, there may be steps to take, but in some situations there is nothing you can do. In the latter, you might ask, "Would you like me to sit with you a while?" There is no one right way to respond to a person at this point, but there are unhelpful responses. We will cover those later in the chapter.

I have already identified the first step of helping: being present and listening. The goal of this first step is to reduce the immediate stress, allow for an expression of feelings, and encourage the person to move from feelings of chaos to order. Many times, the person may be overwhelmed and uncertain what to do next. The second possible step may be helping the person identify initial action steps and assisting them in carrying those out. What steps to take will depend on the situation. For a friend whose spouse has left, we might ask if they feel safe staying in their house. If not, we can help identify a safe place to go. Other people may need to be notified of what has happened, or we might want to help the friend identify professional resources like a counselor or a lawyer. Remember that a person in a situation like this might feel shame (or not yet know how they feel), so do not notify others without the person's request or permission. They may need help with other immediate physical needs like meals or help with getting kids from school. Each situation and circumstance brings unique needs.

Sometimes a person in crisis needs to do the action items themselves, and sometimes other people can do things for them. It is important not to confuse the two. If we are uncertain, it is always appropriate to ask, "What do you need right now?" or "Would it be helpful if I . . . ?" Sometimes a person trying to help may step in, take charge, and start doing or directing. This is appreciated in some situations, but in others it might be overbearing. Some people step in to help because they don't know what else to do. Without listening first, we risk infringing on another person's autonomy. Helping others identify what needs to be done next and doing what we can to facilitate that is an essential step.

When my youngest daughter was nine years old, she had a friend named Jeni who lived two doors down from us. Jeni was an only child, born to her parents after they were told they could not have children. She was their miracle child. One day while playing with friends in the woods behind our house, Jeni pulled on a vine in a tree that brought a loose tree branch down onto her head. She was rushed to the hospital and later died of her injury. Many things happened over the following days and weeks as friends and neighbors tried to help the grieving family. They did not have funds to pay for a funeral for Jeni. One thing we did was organize a yard sale to help raise funds, and we facilitated local news coverage to expand awareness of the need.

In the immediate days after Jeni's death, I noticed that my neighbor's yard needed mowing, so I decided to cut their grass one day after cutting my own yard. I continued to do this over the next weeks until one week, Jeni's father came out and asked, "Why are you cutting my grass?" I was surprised by the emotions that came so easily as I tried to respond to him, but I said, "I don't know what else to do for you, and I feel like I need to do something." The reality was that, if the roles had been reversed, cutting the grass might have been therapeutic for me, and someone else cutting the grass would deprive me of that. What I said to our neighbor was "*I* need to do something." I did not know if this was what they wanted or needed, but I felt powerless in the situation and wanted to do *something*. So I did something. My choice of action was not terrible in this situation, but my motive was more about my need to do something for them than it was about what they might have needed.

When a person in crisis needs encouragement to follow through with a particular next step, our best support might be to ask if they had a chance to do it, ask how it went, or offer to help. We should help people do what they can't do for themselves and not do for them what they can or need to do, at least not without their request or permission. We should also not do more than we are able to do. In some situations, we could hurt ourselves physically, financially, or in other ways trying to fix a problem for someone that is not ours to fix or is better solved by supporting them in their own efforts.

When the Crisis Is Not the Problem

Many people have friends or family members who always seem to be in a crisis. In some cases, it is the same crisis over and over. At some point, we might start to realize that the person in the perpetual crisis is the problem rather than the crisis itself. Our way of help then might be addressing the systemic issue contributing to the perpetual state of crisis instead of trying to bail the person out over and over again.

Edwin Friedman was a student of Murray Bowen's family systems theory and wrote a book called *Generation to Generation* (1985) on Bowen's ideas and how his concepts might apply to church family as well as biological family. Friedman also wrote a small book of fables called *Friedman's Fables* (1990), a collection of stories with a moral or meaning related to a concept of Bowen's theory. One of his fables is called "The Bridge" (1990, 9–13).

"The Bridge" describes a person starting a journey and crossing a long bridge over a deep ravine. The traveling person encounters someone coming from the opposite direction on the bridge. As the two people meet on the bridge, the second person ties a rope around the waist of the first and jumps off the side of the bridge, saying, "Please don't let me fall." As they begin to converse, the second person is clearly asking the first person to be responsible for him by saying, "My life is in your hands," but the first person did not ask for or desire this responsibility. The negotiations continue until the first person finally says, "I will not accept the position of choice for your life, only for my own; the position of choice for your own life I hereby give back to you." He offers to help the one at the end of the rope to climb up, but the dangling person calls him "selfish," telling him, "I *am* your responsibility." When the second person refuses to accept responsibility for himself and climb up, the first person unties the rope from his waist and says, "I accept your decision," releasing the rope.

The ending is dramatic and usually shocking to many with whom I share this story. We want a happy ending where the second person is saved, but the first person does all they can to help. In the end, they cannot save the second person without that person's cooperation. Sometimes such decisions are necessary, and they are never easy.

The Helpful Samaritan

One Bible story that helps conceptualize the idea of helping is often called "The Good Samaritan." In Luke 10:29-37, after Jesus says the greatest command is to love God with your whole being and love your neighbor as yourself, a religious leader asks him, "Who is my neighbor?" The story Jesus tells does not answer that question but a different one: "How am I to be a good neighbor?" The religious leader wants to know to whom he must show love, and Jesus instead says, "This is how you show love." First, Jesus's use of a Samaritan as the helper is key because this people group was undesirable to the Jews of that time. It would be as if a white, straight, Christian man in the United States was beaten by robbers and left to die and then cared for by a Muslim, an immigrant, or a trans man (or a member of any other group that some who claim to be Christian have spoken against in the past several years). For any reader, the identity of the helper should be someone they would have difficulty relating to in another circumstance. The message in Jesus's story is clear: love does not know division. A person in need is a person in need. In order to care for another, we must see them as human beings like we are and do for them as we would want someone to do for us. Jesus says the Samaritan had compassion on the man left for dead. To have compassion, he had to see the injured man as someone like himself and not as a race, nationality, or any other form of difference.

Next, the Samaritan man cares for the injured man with the resources he has: oil and wine. He also puts the man on his own donkey and takes him somewhere safe. The Samaritan does not stay with the injured man until he is well. He uses some of his resources to help pay for the man's care until he is able to return. Then the Samaritan goes to take care of whatever business he has, but he comes later to check on the injured man.

The Samaritan did not give up all of his resources and responsibilities to help the injured man, but his care of this man did cost him something. The Samaritan took time, used resources, and spent money. He was kind and compassionate, but he also left when he needed to and returned when he was able. Being willing to laugh with those who laugh and cry with those who cry involves seeing humanity in the other and setting aside our own needs for the moment in order to help. Helping involves doing what we can for a person that they are currently not able to do for themselves, but it also involves considering our own needs at the same time.

The Nashville Flood of 2010

In May 2010, a two-day weather system flooded many parts of Nashville, destroying businesses and homes. Unnoticed at the time were the dozens of houses like ours and our neighbors' that were not flooded but were severely damaged by mudslides. On May 2, 2010, I stood in my kitchen at the back of our house and watched trees and mud slide down onto my neighbor's house. Looking back on it now, I wonder why we did not have the intelligence to leave our house, but we did not leave. We did, however, move to the basement. The power had been out for a while, and my youngest daughter and I left the house to get lunch for the family. We had not gone a mile down the road when my wife called to say there was a tree in our kitchen. The words did not register at first, and I had to hear them again. "There is a tree in the kitchen!" As it turned out, the mudslide behind our house had not been as dramatic as what happened to our neighbor, but the hill had shifted enough to crack the foundation of our home and send a huge tree through the roof into the kitchen and our youngest daughter's bedroom.

This was indeed a crisis, and we were in shock. The immediate feeling was panic, and my mind raced as I tried to figure out how to process what had happened. I literally walked in circles in our front yard trying to get my thoughts to line up into a coherent plan. I did not know what to do next. As I stood there, neighbors came from different directions on our street with ladders and tarps; some were neighbors I had never met. These friends got the hole in our roof covered within thirty minutes of the incident. The next day, volunteers from two churches came to help remove the tree from the house. We had friends and family offer us a place to stay. Others helped us move. Our belongings were stored in the basements of at least three friends' homes for several months. We were given gift cards for shopping and meals. One anonymous donor gave us a sizeable gift that helped us eventually get into a new home. I cannot name all the friends who helped or all the ways we were helped, but we were blessed by the love and care of others over the weeks and months after that incident.

One incident stayed with me. Early in the aftermath of this incident, a friend called to check on us. He asked if there was anything he could do. I said we had realized that we needed a place to do laundry. My friend replied, "Ok, well, if you need anything, let me know." I don't know if he did not register what I had said or if helping with a place to do laundry was not what he had in mind. He asked what he could do but did not acknowledge our need. It would have been fine for him to say he was not sure they could help in that way. After all, we should help as we are able. However, I have learned that it is best not to offer help if you are not able.

Grief

Grief is a unique form of crisis that deserves special attention because so many things people experience as a crisis involve some kind of loss. The lessons about being helpful in grief apply to other situations of care. Being present with someone in a time of grief means recognizing grief and being comfortable with deep feelings and sadness.

You might think grief should be obvious. Indeed, some losses are easily recognized. We might refer to these as "tangible losses." A tangible loss is when we can observe what has been lost. We may not understand the significance for the other person, but we can see that something that was in their life is no longer there. The death of a friend or family member might be the most obvious, but we can also include the loss of a relationship due to a move, a breakup, divorce, etc. Other losses like the loss of a home or a job (and the income and friends that went with the job) might also seem obvious. I am sure that if you think about yourself or someone you know, you could name other things that would constitute a "tangible loss."

However, there are subtler losses. We would call them "intangible losses" because what is lost is not as obvious. The loss may be so ambiguous that even the person experiencing it may not immediately realize that a loss has occurred and may not connect their emotional distress to the loss. These might include a loss of hopes and dreams tied to vocational aspirations or to other aspirations of any kind. This type of loss might also complicate a tangible loss in that the loss of a relationship or a person might be obvious, but the ways the tangible loss affects an individual may also include intangible losses. For example, a parent who experiences a miscarriage or the loss of a child obviously has the tangible loss of that child, but there is also the intangible loss of the hopes, dreams, and expectations for a future. People can experience a loss of security after surviving a crime or when a person is stalked. Loss of identity might be another intangible loss (not in the sense of identity theft, although that might carry a form of grief as well, but the loss of identity in the sense of losing who we understood ourselves to be), as a person might have to come to grips with revelations that shatter their sense of self and confront the reality of who they are. Loss of faith is another loss. Sometimes it may be the complete loss of faith, or it may be the loss of faith that was narrower in exchange for something more expansive. At times there may be nostalgia for a simpler, black-and-white faith when confronted with a large moral dilemma. Again, this list is not comprehensive, and you may be able identify other such losses you have experienced.

Whether a person identifies with a religion or not, any significant loss can challenge their underlying beliefs. Some losses cause a person to feel unmoored and unstable. Amid such loss, it is tempting to try to suppress or avoid uncertainty and pain. However, grief is not something we can avoid. We have to find a way to deal with grief or grief will deal with us. Unprocessed grief affects our mood, our other relationships, our future relationships, and/or our sense of peace and well-being. Being present with someone experiencing grief can help create space for grieving that leads to healing, or it can drive a person inward with shame and loneliness that leads to more emotional distress. To better understand how to be present, it is helpful to understand more about the process of grieving.

The States of Grief

Elizabeth Kübler-Ross's famous "Stages of Grief" (denial, anger, bargaining, depression, acceptance) are now ubiquitous. However, the familiarity of these stages means that people regularly misuse, misapply, or misunderstand them. I will add context to these stages that might guide you in helping someone in grief (or perhaps help you understand your own grieving process).

I once heard someone describe the stages of grief using the experience of a car that would not start. Suppose you go out one morning and get in your car to go somewhere. You put your key in the ignition or press the start button and nothing happens. The first thing you do is try again (and maybe again and again). This reflects *denial*: "This can't be happening" or "This isn't real." What you feel next might vary, but at some point you might feel *anger*: "What is wrong with this stupid car?" "I can't be late today. I have too much going on." For this scenario, *bargaining* might look like us talking to the car: "Come on, baby, I just need you to start one time. I can take you to the shop later, but I have to get to work right now. Just start for me one time!" Ultimately, we feel overwhelmed and *depressed* that our day is not going as we planned, and we reach *acceptance* when we finally pick up the phone and call a tow truck.

The reality, however, is that grief is not linear. Grief does not follow steps or stages, and it is not progressive, which is why I refer to them as "states of grief" and not "stages." A person may feel any one of these states at any time. They may experience more than one at a time and may not experience one or more of them. Grief is not predictable, and it is not uniform. Each person's grief is unique. As we listen to a person share their experiences, we can listen for various states, but we don't need to anticipate or prescribe them. When they are present, the experience can be as unique as the person grieving. Below are some ways to listen for these various states of grief.

Denial of a loss can take many forms, from blatantly refusing to accept reality to feeling disbelief. This difficulty accepting the reality of a loss can exist even as a person deals with the other parts of the grief response. Again, these are not progressive; they are states of being that overlap, wax and wane, and morph over time. To be adequately present with someone in a state of denial, we should offer empathy for the disbelief and not challenge the reality. We don't have to tell someone, "You know this is real" or "You know you're going to have to deal with this sometime." Instead, we can offer words of understanding: "I know it's so hard to believe this is real."

Similarly, anger can take many forms. At the heart of a person's anger is an attempt to make sense of a loss and understand why something has happened or why this has happened to them. A person may have a sense of righteous anger as they wrestle with how unfair the situation is, how undeserving a person was for what happened, or how undeserving they may feel for having to deal with the aftermath of the loss. This sense of anger is fueled when the person feels a sense of injustice over the loss. This may be more likely to happen if a person does not have a belief system that allows for such tragedies. However, sometimes a loss can make people question beliefs they thought were secure. Anger may also reflect the loss of expectations and plans for what a person believed was supposed to be versus the reality they live now. This may be expressed in the feeling that a person's life was taken too soon. Or a grieving person might express anger at someone or some entity that they perceive (justly or unjustly) to be the cause of the loss. This is part of the grieving person's attempt answer the question "Why?" and to make sense of something that feels meaningless. The blame may be focused on a hospital, a negligent entity, criminal activity, God, and even the dead person (i.e., "How could you do this to me?"). In such situations, the better response is not to defend God or others who may be blamed but simply to empathize with the feeing being expressed. The grieving person may know the answer to their own struggles, but the act of blaming is part of a process that needs to occur before they can reach a place of acceptance.

Elizabeth Kübler-Ross initially worked with terminally ill patients who were wrestling with acceptance of their diagnosis and death. In this context, the concept of "bargaining" makes more sense. Bargaining is often expressed as some variation of "If I do X, then you will do Y" or "I promise to do X if you will only do Y." A loved one might think or pray, "If I could trade places with him/her, I would." After a loss, bargaining might involve phrases like "What if" or "If only." People recount the events and wonder, "If I had done this thing instead of that thing, they might still be here," or "Why did I choose to do this or that? Things might have turned out differently." In some cases, this may reflect a person's justifiable need to face how they contributed to a situation, but in other cases, it is merely an attempt to make sense of why events unfolded in a certain way. Bargaining reflects a struggle for acceptance. It is an attempt to have a sense of control in a situation that is out of control.

While Christians might think of bargaining in terms of prayer to God, even people who do not believe that God operates in this way and people who don't believe in God at all may pray in times of grief. Bargaining is an attempt to restore order to a situation that seems chaotic. It reflects a resistance to accept what is happening. Accepting a loss changes us, and it is human nature to resist profound change. Again, a person wrestling with grief does not need a theology lesson about how God operates or even an affirmation that God will accomplish something good. If we respond at all, we should simply reflect the underlying feeling of helplessness without rushing to fix it.

The state of grief that is called "depression" may or may not fit the criteria for a formal diagnosis. Whether it does or not is less significant than the feelings a person experiences. They may feel and express feelings of deep sadness and a sense of helplessness and/or hopelessness. They may have difficulty sleeping, or they may sleep more than usual. They may lose their appetite or eat more than usual. They may not have energy to do anything, and they may lose interest in doing things they used to enjoy. Such feelings may cause others to feel uncomfortable, but it is important not to try to move people out of this state. Allowing ourselves and others to feel the fullness of feelings associated with a particular loss is a critical part of healing.

Many people are uncomfortable with feelings of sadness in themselves or in others. Because of this, a person may discourage another's sadness, try to make them feel better by saying "happy things," or try to hurry a process of grieving along: "Aren't you over that yet?" Some people believe that people of faith should be upbeat and positive and see sadness as the opposite of being faithful. Some people avoid expressing sadness and say they are trying to "be strong" for someone else. True strength, however, allows us (and others) to fully feel sadness. It requires being with people who are grieving, not trying to move them out of sadness. This means we must first work through our own grief and sadness and then manage our discomfort in order to be in the presence of another who is devastated. We cannot be fully present with someone in grief if we are not comfortable with sadness.

While "acceptance" might seem to need no explanation, I think it does because people have varying understandings of what it means to accept a loss. Acceptance is not "getting over it" but learning to live into a future without what is lost. When a loved one dies, acceptance is learning to love in the absence of that loved one. Living with grief means living with a scar that others may not be able to see. We are forever affected, and grief is never fully over.

To be clear, acceptance is not a perpetual state but a cyclical experience. A person may seem to accept a loss or a situation one minute and then return to anger and denial the next. Acceptance is an ongoing process, not an event. This is true for many reasons, but one common struggle is a fear of forgetting or losing what is left behind. A person may fear that they are not honoring the lost person or their memory if they begin to live a new life. Some people may also be fearful to move on when they have only known life one way or with a particular person. They may not be able to conceptualize living without that person present. (The loss may not be a person. For example, someone who is retiring from a lifetime of a particular work may have difficulty conceptualizing a life that does not involve doing that work.) At this point in grief, some people get stuck. Be aware of your responses. Recognize that the cyclical nature of states of grief is normal. Returning to another state of grief is not regression; it is part of the process. Normalizing this rather than saying, "I thought you were over it," is helpful. People often come to counseling with grief, and they say they need a place to talk about their feelings because their friends are "tired of listening" to them. In some cases, this has been true, as some people don't know how to deal with prolonged grief. However, in other cases, the person coming to counseling may simply fear overwhelming their friends. Offering to be present as long as grief takes is a generous and wonderful gift to a friend who is grieving.

What Not to Say

When someone we know is grieving or in some form of distress, it can be difficult to know what to say or do. It is helpful to learn what *not* to say:

"I know how you feel." Even if you have been through something similar, you cannot know exactly what another person is feeling, and most people will feel anger at such statements because they want to feel their own feelings and express their own experience. If you have truly been through something similar, you might say that but add, "I don't know what your experience of this might be." If you attempt such a response, be sure that your experience is comparable. You don't want to say, "I know what it's like to have a heart attack because I went to the ER once with a cut on my finger."

"There is a reason for everything" or *"It's all part of God's plan."* Any trite statement or cliché is generally unhelpful. While it might help us feel that we are offering something to comfort the person's pain, they may or may not ultimately find meaning in their loss. If they do, it will take time. Either way, people must discover meaning or purpose in a tragedy on their own. We cannot give it to them.

"He/she is in a better place." While a grieving person may believe this, saying it to them does not change how deeply they miss someone.

"You can always . . . remarry, have another child, get another pet, etc." We can never replace something dear that is lost. We can learn to live with the loss, and we may learn to love and connect again, but we will always miss what we lost. Having another spouse, child, job, dog, etc., does not replace the memory or remove the grief. We just learn to live with the loss and find new joy.

"This is behind you now; it's time to get on with your life" or *"That was so long ago; aren't you over it yet?"* Grief takes as long as it takes for a person, and each person grieves in their own way.

"You should do this" or *"You shouldn't feel that."* Any directive statement is probably more about our own discomfort and/or our desire to try to fix the problem than about the person's grief.

Ways to Help

It is also helpful to learn what to say or do when a person grieves:

"I don't know how you feel, but I'm here to help any way I can." Do not offer to help if you don't mean it, but if you do, it is often better to offer to do specific things because grieving people can't always think about more mundane needs. Remember to always ask permission.

"I wish I had something to say that could make it better, but know I care about you." It is better to say you don't know what to say than to say something you think might make someone feel better. In reality, whatever you might say probably can't make it better, and the person just needs someone to be with them at that moment.

Say nothing. Instead of trying to say the "right thing," offer someone a hug. If you sit with them, be comfortable with silence; don't try to fill it. Allow them to tell you the story of how their loved one died or about their loss. Every telling of that story helps.

Don't rush grief. Grieving takes as long as it takes, and people express grief in many ways.

Mind the special occasions. The first year after a loss can be particularly difficult with the "first" holiday, birthday, etc. without the loved one. Offer extra support at those times and over time. Remember most people will offer care and support only until the funeral is over. It can be meaningful for someone to be remembered well beyond that time.

Facilitate memories and storytelling. The goal for grieving is attachment, not detachment from what is lost. Ask questions to facilitate memories and stories. Share your own memories and stories about a person or experience. Memories can facilitate laughter and sadness, and grief involves both.

Ritualize memories. One way to facilitate memories is to create special rituals that facilitate connection to what or who is lost. This might be lighting a candle on a particular anniversary, preparing food from a recipe passed down from a family member, or putting a special ornament on the Christmas tree. The action connects us to the memory and feelings.

Directing Friends to Other Resources

We want to be available to our friends in a time of crisis, loss, or tragedy, and we can always make ourselves available to listen to someone share their experiences. However, sometimes what a friend shares might indicate the need for more help than we can provide. In such times, our best help might be to assist our friend in identifying appropriate resources and supporting them in following up. There are at least four such situations that are common.

First, the person shares something that is life-threatening, such as issues of addiction, abuse, or suicidal thoughts. As discussed in previous chapters, a friend might share something that we have obligation to report to authorities, such as the abuse of a child. As an alternative, we might encourage our friend to report some things themselves and offer support as they do that. In the case of addiction, we may not need to do something immediately, but generally if a friend shares concerns about their own use of a substance, they are probably ready to consider help. Offering to help find resources or support the friend while they call someone for assistance is appropriate. I cannot adequately cover the topic of suicidality in this chapter. However, a person expressing something passive like "I wish I had never been born" or "No one would care if I died" is fairly common. By itself, it does not necessarily mean they are at risk of taking their own life, but it is important to follow up: "Are you thinking about killing yourself?" If the person is not thinking about this, they will make that clear, and asking the question will not push them in that direction. If they are thinking about suicide, your question may provide relief because they consciously or unconsciously want someone to know and to help them find assistance. Any time someone hints at suicide or mentions suicide, it should be taken seriously.

I once had a client who often called me between sessions for things that did not feel like a crisis. I talked to her about this, but she continued. I finally set a limit on how much she called me and said suicidality was a reason for her to call. Her calls came less frequently but regularly included talk of suicide. She had not realized that I would take such talk seriously, and I tried to get her to go to the emergency room or call the local mobile crisis unit. She asked why I was doing that, and I clarified that I was taking her talk of suicide seriously. Ultimately, she admitted that she felt anxious between our sessions and wanted to connect with me, but she was not suicidal. Even if you have doubts about a person's motivation, never take talk of suicide lightly.

A second situation requiring extra resources is when a friend has the same crisis again and again, or we see them struggling with an issue without apparent progress. We can express our observations and concerns. "You statements" like "You're not getting better" or "You keep having the same trouble over and over" may not be well received. We might say something like, "You dealt with this issue last year, and it came up earlier this year, and now you're dealing with it again. I'm concerned that this is something that might need more help than I can offer you as friend. Could I help you find someone who might be able to help so you don't have to struggle this way?" If you are evaluating a person's "lack of progress," be sure the issue is not just that you are uncomfortable with the other person's emotions. You might point to concrete events and provide your own observations, avoiding speculation. Express your thoughts as concerns for the other and perhaps explore their interest in getting help. You might say, "I notice that you had this trouble in X situation, and it seems that this is the same thing that has now affected you in y situation. Do you think it might be helpful to talk to someone who knows about such things and could help you better deal with this?"

Third, a friend might present you with a situation that you know nothing about. Perhaps they express a need for social services that you have not utilized before, or they talk about a situation to which you have never been exposed. In such cases, it is ok to say, "I'm sorry you're in this situation. I'm happy for you to talk to me about what's going on. I'm also wondering if it would be ok for me to help you find someone who might know more about this and could help us find the right resources to help."

Years ago, I met a person struggling with classic symptoms of obsessive-compulsive disorder (OCD). I had not worked with anyone with these symptoms prior to meeting this person, so I presented my work with this client to my supervisor. My supervisor gave me a way to assess that I was dealing with OCD but also observed that the therapy in which I was primarily trained would not be helpful for such a person. (A person with OCD does not respond to insight-oriented or psychodynamic therapy.) With my supervisor's assistance, I identified a clinic that dealt specifically with issues of OCD. I talked to my client about this and gave her the information for the OCD clinic. The client promised to follow up with the clinic. I did not verify this but hoped that she would. Years later, I had a chance meeting with her at an event in the area. She approached me and asked if I remembered her. I confirmed that I did and then she said, "You saved my life." I was shocked because I had not provided direct assistance and had only referred her to what I hoped would be a good resource. This person confirmed that her experience at the OCD clinic was miraculously helpful, and she was so much better. Helping connect others with the appropriate resources can be as helpful as (or more helpful than) trying to provide assistance that we are not trained to provide.

Fourth, the person shares something that is overwhelming to us. They may talk about something traumatic that is more than our ability to tolerate, or they may share something that is like our own experience. If we have not adequately healed from what we went through, our friend's story may activate strong emotional responses or reactions in us. This will probably inhibit our ability to be helpful to our friend but is also an indication that we have healing work to do for ourselves.

One final note: it is not your job to determine what is going on with a struggling friend or relative. It is definitely not your job to determine a diagnosis for someone. Even if you have experience with a particular diagnosis, and what you see in your friend could be that, it may not be. Suggesting treatments, medications, supplements, or other help could potentially be dangerous. Again, you can observe what you see or experience and encourage a friend to seek appropriate help. You can encourage them and support them in getting help, but trying to diagnose someone without proper training could do more harm than good.

Summary

There are many events and experiences that people consider crises, but what constitutes a crisis can vary from person to person. This is partially due to the meaning a person makes of a particular event because of their previous experience(s). It can also depend on the internal and external resources a person has in their life to help them cope.

The first way to help someone experiencing a crisis is to be present and listen. We model our presence on the God who loved us so much that God took our form in order to experience life as we do. Being present with someone experiencing a crisis is an embodiment of God's presence. We should not move too quickly to try to fix the other person or the situation but instead spend time listening and facilitating the person's sharing. This allows them to identify and process feelings, begin to make meaning of what has happened, and experience the care of someone willing to hear their story. Once we believe we understand the situation, we can help them develop a plan of action. There may ways for us to offer help, or we may need to support the person as they do what they need to do. When we offer to help, we should only offer what we are able and willing to do. These should be specific tasks, as the other person may not yet know what will be helpful. And we should ask permission to help before we do anything.

While it is reasonable for friends to be willing to inconvenience themselves to help one another, helping others should always be balanced with our own ability and care of ourselves. We should not try to do for others what another person is more qualified to do, and we should not do for someone what they want or need to do for themselves. Hurting ourselves while helping another only escalates the situation and will not bring resolution. If we exhaust ourselves trying to help, then we are ultimately not able to continue being helpful.

Finally, many events that we experience as a crisis involve some form of grief. Many tangible losses also include intangible elements of loss. Intangible losses can be the primary cause of a crisis, and a person may require support to identify the underlying contributing factors. While there may be similarities in how people grieve, each person grieves in the time and way that is necessary for them to heal. There are things we can do to facilitate healing, and there are things that are ultimately not helpful. It is important to understand the difference if we truly want to be present with someone in a crisis.

We must allow the other person the autonomy to do their own work, help them identify outside resources when necessary, and take care of ourselves. Remember that you are not obligated to help another person, and you are not responsible for their healing. Choosing to be present with someone in need is a gift, and supporting another person as they find healing is meaningful. Often our attempts to control outcomes, fix things for others, or hurry another's process are more about our own discomfort and need than about being helpful.

Chapter 8

Friendship Lifecycle

The process of psychotherapy has a beginning (intake and assessment), a middle (working phase), and an end (termination). In an ideal situation, termination comes after spending adequate time in the previous two phases to assist a client in accomplishing their therapy goals. For me, this is not just about reducing or resolving the "symptoms" that brought the client to therapy but helping them develop internal awareness and resources that will assist them with novel situations and challenges and hopefully bring a transformative experience of relationship with themselves, others, and the eternal. This process takes as long as it takes. For some, just a session or two can be helpful in restabilizing a historically balanced life. For others, a long-term relationship with a therapist may be necessary to accomplish goals of overcoming childhood traumas or deep characterological challenges. The code of ethics for most professional therapists has a clause that prevents a therapist from seeing a client if they believe the therapy is not beneficial. However, for some, "beneficial" may mean having a person in their life who offers them the support and care they do not find elsewhere. For others, "beneficial" means moving toward specific life goals. A long-term relationship involving the client's deep and productive work can be meaningful for both client and therapist. However, like all relationships, therapy comes to an end, and handling the ending well is important.

One of my supervisors first introduced me to the concept that every "hello" has an implied "goodbye." The hello may be to a person we will see for a few minutes at a supermarket checkout or on an elevator, or it may be a person with whom we share a decades-long, deep, and intimate relationship that ends when one person dies. The length of time that people are connected, the quality of the relationship, and the nature of the ending all affect the experience of the goodbye. A relationship may end in a way that feels premature but be profoundly meaningful, while others may end after a long connection without significant consequence. A good relationship deserves a good "goodbye" that celebrates what has been good and acknowledges the value of the connection. A less than ideal relationship may end with intentionality but may not be something to celebrate, and some relationships may end without any acknowledgment.

In my years of working as a pastoral therapist, I have ended several therapeutic relationships well. When a client realizes that they have accomplished what they intended (or more than they intended) in therapy and feel comfortable trying "to fly" without the regular support of a therapist, it is important to have at least one session to reflect on the progress the person has made, think about concerns they might have as they leave, and appreciate the resources they are taking with them. Because therapists invest a great deal of themselves into relationships with clients over a period of time, they may have feelings of sadness about therapy ending, but they may also feel gratitude for the time, pride for the accomplishments, satisfaction in the environment they have co-created that resulted in success, and more.

In my years as a chaplain, I had the opportunity to be with several patients and their loved ones who had to say goodbye to one another for the last time. In one situation, an older gentleman gently stroked his wife's hair as she was dying and said to her, "You have been such a good friend to me. I'm going to miss you." In that moment, I was inspired to live a life in which such a scene might be possible for me. I was also aware of how many others do not have the emotional capacity to connect with such a depth of sadness and miss the potential for significant connection. As we saw in the previous chapter, loving another person well means being vulnerable to deep sadness in death and loss.

However, a therapeutic relationship might end prematurely for several reasons. We have touched on some of these, like empathic failure, in previous chapters, but I want to address others more specifically because I believe there are potential parallels in friendships and other relationships. In an article about treating what is now known as dissociative identity disorder, Richard Kluft outlined a process of therapy that has universal applications. He identified several scenarios in which continuation of therapy may not be advisable or in which a "positive outcome is unlikely" (1993, 152). To simplify, these are some reasons that a therapeutic relationship might be terminated prior to all goals being achieved. Many of these might also apply to other relationships outside of professional psychotherapy.

Failure to Establish a Therapeutic Alliance

I recently had an initial visit with a client in which I did what I outlined in previous chapters to build connections and be sure that I understood the client's concerns. Toward the end of the session, I outlined the therapeutic process in which I imagined we could engage and how I thought it might address his concerns. He agreed to return for another session, but prior to that second session, he called and left a message for me saying he did not feel that we would be a good fit. It seemed that he had different ideas of what the therapy should look like or of what he wanted, and we failed to make that connection. This happens occasionally, and I understand it intellectually, but I always feel sad that I am not able to be of help to every person. Sometimes it takes a few sessions to discover that what I have to offer as a therapist may not be a good fit or that my style does not work for a particular client. Ultimately, the client decides not to come back because we do not make the connection required for a working relationship.

This seems similar to when I have coffee or lunch with a potential new friend, and we don't connect at the level I had hoped. As noted previously, it may be because this person is not looking for a new friend, is unable to have the deep conversations I desire, or simply don't have the time. It might be that our personalities clash in a way that makes communication difficult or awkward. Regardless, while we may have connections in another aspect of life, the transition to a deeper friendship does not seem possible. This is not because either of us or wrong or bad; it just is. So a deeper relationship might end before it has a chance to begin.

Disagreement about Process

As I described in a previous chapter, some people come to counseling with fears about what it will be like or with ideas of what they want, so from the first meeting they try to control the process of therapy. They may say with words or their actions, "I want you to help me, but we will not talk about X," or "I want you to help me, and you should do it this way." There is a process to therapy, and each therapist, because of their own training, supervision, theoretical orientation, and personality, will do therapy differently. While there may be "wrong ways" to do therapy, there is no one right way to do it. Clients must be able to trust the process of therapy. Often, if they simply let the process be what it is, it can lead to great outcomes. I have sat with many clients over the years who have refused to practice new tools we have talked about in the therapy room or to participate in various conversations or exercises and then complained that therapy is not (or I am not) helping. There is vulnerability in going to therapy. It takes courage to open yourself to an uncomfortable process and potentially examine things you have worked hard to suppress, hide, or ignore. I understand why this is difficult. However, when fear or concerns about doing the work interfere with the process, the ultimate success of therapy may be sabotaged.

Similarly, in friendships there may be people who subtly or not so subtly try to control the relationship. Time together always occurs on their schedule or always occurs in one way. A friend might avoid a more intimate time together in exchange for time at an event with limited opportunities for deeper interaction. A friend may only show up for us at certain times or for certain things but otherwise avoid time together. A friend may feel so strongly about certain issues that they do not think they can have a friendship with someone who holds a different view. This is an inability to let go of how they think things are supposed to be in favor of trying to control the content and process of the relationship. If one person continually tries (consciously or unconsciously) to control how a relationship unfolds, it will not have the potential to be all that it might otherwise be. The person who fears vulnerability in a relationship may act to keep the relationship in an emotional place that feels safe. It will be difficult for the relationship to progress beyond that point.

Violation of Boundaries

In the way that Kluft uses the term "violation of boundaries," it means the client's continued violation of the therapist's boundaries, especially ones that are established and clarified. As a client, if your therapist regularly violated the professional boundaries of psychotherapy, it would be a sign to find a different therapist (and perhaps report the therapist to the regulatory boards). In the case of a client violating boundaries, however, most therapists present them with a document or statement of boundaries regarding issues like phone calls outside the session, emails, text messages, social media, etc. This helps establish the frame of therapy. The first time a client violates such a boundary, the therapist may need to remind them of the boundary. There are times when a client behaves in a problematic way that the therapist did not anticipate, and a boundary needs to be established or more firmly established.

In my practice, I have been open to having phone calls from clients between sessions if they are experiencing something "urgent," but I generally limit such phone calls to non-emergency issues and to calls that are briefer in nature. A hypothetical client could use the knowledge that I will return a phone call to make a connection outside sessions but want to talk about an issue that could or should be discussed in a session. A client may want to talk about an issue that is more of a crisis than a brief phone call can handle. A client may send a "content-related message" after I have clarified that email and texts, for the most part, should be used only for scheduling issues. There is generally no ill intent on the part of the client, and the breach of boundaries simply requires a conversation with them.

In the movie *What about Bob*, the patient named Bob (Bill Murray) insinuates himself into the life of his psychiatrist, Dr. Leo Marvin (Richard Dreyfuss). This is humorous because of its absurdity, but some therapists have had to fear for their lives because of clients who become obsessed with them, stalk them, and eventually threaten them. Such gross violations or a series of minor violations are definitely conditions under which a therapist may terminate therapy. For the relationship to work, both parties have to feel safe, and the frame of therapy helps establish that sense of safety.

I know there are stories about friendships that have gone horribly wrong in similar ways, but most of us may have only experienced this in less dramatic ways. While we may enjoy the company of a particular friend, they may show up uninvited, make assumptions about their inclusion in certain events, or cross boundaries by talking to other friends about us or our relationships. Being able to discuss how this makes you uncomfortable is essential for keeping the friendship good, avoiding resentment, and preventing any escalation of behaviors. However, there are definitely times when it might feel more comfortable to end a relationship because of such violations, especially after other conversations about a problematic behavior. When it feels safe to do so, offering a friend feedback about why you are limiting interaction or ending a relationship might be helpful as they hopefully continue to grow in self-awareness.

I want to offer a word of caution, however. In the same way that the frame of therapy is designed to create a safe, healing environment, healthy boundaries are designed to move us to health and wholeness. Healthy boundaries with others should help us safely be close to another person. Unfortunately, boundaries can sometimes be treated as a way to protect ourselves and focus on what and who we keep out of our lives. Notice the difference.

Healthy boundaries can be expressed with great love and compassion. However, too often people allow their boundaries to be violated multiple times before they even try to set any, so when they finally attempt to set a boundary, they are angry and may be unnecessarily extreme. Boundaries can and should be focused, as much as possible, on what is encouraged or allowed and not just on what is not desired. Sometimes we might attempt to set boundaries not around health and wholeness but simply around comfort. If we don't like people to disagree with us or we find opposing views or opinions threatening, we might try to "set a boundary" around another person's freedom of expression. Just because we don't like what they are saying does not mean they have no right to say it. Open and honest communication is a hallmark of healthy relationships. Trying to "set a boundary" about what another person can say or do may not be in the service of health and wholeness. An emotionally unhealthy person may sometimes try to "set boundaries" that limit the capacity for connection by attempting to control another person and limit their own emotional vulnerability. Boundaries should be carefully considered. In relationships, they may be co-created to accomplish a common purpose of safe and healthy interaction.

Failure to Attend Therapy or Do the Work

At times in therapy, clients have said that they are ready to engage in a process of therapy and have agreed to the framework of a therapeutic relationship, but then they begin to miss appointments regularly. Similarly, clients may say they want help but regularly fail to reflect on our sessions between meetings or fail to practice new behaviors, etc. in their life. If a client continues to miss appointments or never seems to be engaged in the process, a therapist should look for an opportunity to check in with the client to see how they feel about the work they are doing. If the client regularly has difficulty making time for the sessions, struggles to remember the sessions, or does not regularly reflect on the conversations of therapy between meetings, this might indicate that the person is not as committed to the process as they might have verbally stated in early sessions. A therapist might terminate therapy in such a case, or sometimes bringing the concern to the client's attention may cause them to acknowledge their feelings and voluntarily withdraw. Sometimes, though, bringing this to a client's attention can help them confront feelings that they are not yet consciously aware of, and that can facilitate therapy moving forward in a more productive way.

I have already acknowledged that I can sometimes be a "bad friend" in that I get busy and may not spend enough time with friends. The reality is that my mental health generally suffers if I am not spending time with friends with whom I can share openly and honestly, and while I might withdraw for a time, I will come back around and seek to engage my friends. However, there are people who might agree that they would like to have a deeper relationship and that they need a good friend, but then they regularly forget the meetings, arrive late, or fail to make contact between meetings. As indicated in chapter 6, such behaviors may reflect unacknowledged and unspoken resistance to the relationship. This might present an opportunity to end a relationship. If we do not understand what the other person feels or thinks, we might spend too much time trying to accommodate and engage the other person when there is no potential for a good future together. But having a "process-oriented" conversation about such issues might help move the relationship to a place of greater openness and honesty.

Abusive Language (or Attitudes) Beyond My Tolerance

Kluft describes this in a way that might fit the context of repeated violation of boundaries, but I want to treat it as a separate issue for a particular reason. In therapy, a client should feel that they can "show up" however they are. They may use profanity at times to express deep feelings. There are times when client may not understand the process of therapy, or therapy stirs up something uncomfortable for them and they push back on it. In many cases, the understanding, non-reactive response of a therapist can help the client process their feelings, move to a new awareness, and communicate more effectively.

However, some clients might seek to control the process of therapy by acting or speaking in an intimidating or abusive manner to the therapist. Simply because a therapist desires to be helpful does not mean they should allow abuse. Kluft says, "It is countertherapeutic to allow oneself to be abused by the patient" (1993, 152), meaning the client gets no therapeutic benefit when a therapist allows them to behave in the office the same way they behave in other parts of their life. It is not a good example to accept such abuse without any feedback or attempt to engage. In some cases, a person's intention is such that there is no engagement and no respect for established boundaries. In such cases, termination of therapy is a necessary part of the therapy for the client and the therapist.

No relationship is served when one person exercises control and manipulation of the other person. Whether done by verbal abuse, emotional manipulation, or physical intimidation, there is no place for such behavior in a meaningful relationship. A relationship that includes such dynamics is not a relationship of mutuality and will not be mutually beneficial. Once a person makes an unsuccessful attempt to bring this behavior to the other's attention, there is generally nothing that will change the behavior. Repeated attempts to talk the person out of their behavior are futile and ill advised. We have different levels of tolerance for certain behaviors, but we should not continue to be in relationship with someone who continually exceeds our tolerance for those behaviors.

Healthy Boundaries & Necessary Losses

In the context of relationships, there are times when people talk about "necessary losses." Repeated attempts to heal contentious relationships have failed because at least one party refuses to acknowledge wrongdoing, continues to justify their abusive behavior, or even fails to recognize there is a problem. In such cases, for the sanity, safety, and health of others in the relationship, a relationship should be ended. For romantic relationships where this type of behavior is present, ending them usually requires professional guidance and intervention because of the potential for physical violence. A "necessary loss," however, happens when there is a movement toward health and wholeness in a person, relationship, or organization, and the one preventing health and wholeness is not willing or able to recognize their participation in the problem.

Other Reasons Relationships End

A relationship that feels like it ends prematurely can still be meaningful. In the sections above, we looked at reasons one or both parties in a relationship might choose to end a relationship or limit interaction. Relationships end for a variety of reasons. Most of those are more benign than the things discussed so far. Probably the most common reason does not involve a formal ending at all. Many relationships do not have a formal ending or an opportunity for goodbye. At some point, we realize that we are not spending as much time with a particular person as we used to. We might say we have "drifted apart." This drift in a relationship can occur for several reasons.

A common reason for drift relates to time and proximity. Relationships require time, and because of our proximity to people in certain circles or circumstances, we spend more time with them. We may take a class related to a hobby, attend a particular Sunday school class at church, take our kids to the same athletic activities, attend the same professional meetings, etc. In each context, we may have the opportunity to meet and interact with others and possibly develop good relationships over time. As our circumstances change, though, we may no longer be involved in the same activities. We might move or our children grow up and move on to other schools or activities. We might change hobbies, change cities, change jobs, change churches, etc. Because of this, it becomes more challenging to maintain relationships with those from the previous context. We might find that over time, we are meeting new people in our new context, and it is hard to maintain all the relationships in the same way we did before. I heard or read years ago that our social relationships change about every five years. Certain friends might transcend the decades, but many of our connections are based in our contexts and change when the contexts change.

This does not mean the relationships were not good; they may have been meaningful during the time we had them. We may feel a sense of sadness and grieve what we have lost, but this does not mean it is any easier to maintain or recapture the previous experience. In many cases, the shared context and shared experience is part of what binds us together. We can feel nostalgic for those times, but the context and shared experience no longer exists.

As I wrote the section of the book about my friendship with Kyle Cantrell, I contacted him about using the story of our relationship in this book. I shared with him what I had written. He said reading my description caused him to miss the time we had. For a period of several years, Kyle and I met regularly for lunch. Over time, I changed jobs, and he changed jobs. He changed churches, and eventually my wife and I changed churches. Our work schedules made getting together more difficult. We were not regularly seeing each other in our shared context. At first, we didn't meet as often, and then we didn't meet. Those years of lunch with Kyle were important in my personal development. I learned a great deal about myself and how to be in a good relationship. I am grateful for my friendship with Kyle. I am sad now that I don't have the connection with him. Because of that relationship (and others), I have learned to have better relationships and have developed subsequent meaningful friendships. The fact that we are friends in different ways than we were previously does not discount the importance of that relationship for me or the importance of Kyle as a friend.

Drift in relationships can occur in other ways as schedules, distance, and priorities shift over time and the shared connection gets more difficult to maintain. Another significant drifting may not be acknowledged. Many people become friends at a particular time in their lives. They are struggling with challenges unique to a particular phase of life. They may hold certain views or beliefs. They may conceptualize parenting, work, faith, etc. in a particular way. Sometimes people form relationships with others with the expectation that the others will never change, but people do change. The changes people experience are not always for the better, but people are always changing. New information, new circumstances, and new challenges or crises can challenge existing beliefs, understandings, or ways of being. As one person grows and changes in a certain way, some friends may not be able to accept or accommodate the changes. Relationships, including with our significant other, reach moments when one or both parties have changed, and the challenge to the previous relationship forces the current relationship to grow and change or end.

Two people may bond over their shared faith experience. They may talk regularly about their understanding of Scripture, their experience of the holy in their lives, etc. However, if one person ultimately begins to question some of the foundational beliefs of the faith that they have shared, the relationship may not be able to accommodate the change. One friend might confess to the other that they are having doubts and questions. The friend might respond with traditional beliefs and responses to try to shore up the other person's faith, or they might offer empathy for the experience of doubt. However, if one friend moves from the shared faith conversations and the relationship cannot tolerate the change, the friends may wind up spending time with others with whom they share more in common.

Two friends may have met young and bonded over drinking and going to clubs together. As one of them begins to confront concerns about their use of alcohol while the other does not, it can create strain and distance in the relationship. For some, a conversation about their feelings and individual experiences might allow them to grow together in a new understanding or a new way of being. However, many times, one friend moves toward health while the other is not ready or able to move in the same direction, and the relationship ends. Unfortunately, the opposite of such a scenario may also be true as one friend descends into greater alcohol abuse and the other grows more and more concerned for them. After many conversations and attempts to support the friend who is struggling, the relationship may lose mutuality and end.

There is no way to cover every conceivable reason that friendships drift or end. However, I think it is important to acknowledge that this happens. It is not necessarily a bad thing when it does. Often it just happens. As discussed in previous chapters, sometimes breaks in relationship require an attempt to understand the rift and possibly make amends. Other times, there is no one event, or neither friend has done anything wrong, but the relationship just does not function as it once did. When possible, it seems healthy to acknowledge the significance of such relationships and celebrate what has been, but obviously that is not always possible. We do not always know when a visit may be the last that we will have someone.

Everyone and Nobody

I would like to offer a word of caution that I hope might prompt specific self-reflection. If in the course of your life, you find that you regularly begin a sentence with "Everyone is . . ." or "Nobody ever . . . ," you might need self-reflection. If you feel like everyone in your life (or in the world) is trying to take advantage of you; that everyone looks down on you; that everyone around you is dumber than you; that everyone around you is smarter than you; that nobody cares about you; that nobody is interested in what you have to say; that everyone angers you; that nobody does things the right way or thinks about the proper way to do things, then there is a strong possibility that the problem is not with other people. If such things regularly come to your mind, the struggle you have may be with yourself and not with others. It is easier to look at what we think others do wrong or to see others' struggles than to look at ourselves honestly. It is tempting to try to tell others how we think they should be or what they are doing wrong, but ultimately, we do not have control over what others do, and a shift needs to occur in us.

Jesus seems to have such things in mind when he says we should not judge one another. His encouragement to take note of the "plank" in our own eye before we focus on a "speck" we see in our brother's eye (Matt 7:3-5) acknowledges that our struggles may affect how we perceive other people. It is easier to see the difficulties others have than it is to look at our own problems. In my experience, I find that once I address some of my struggles and issues, I become less concerned about the difficulties of others; when I do try to help another person, I can do so from a place of greater empathy and humility. Self-reflection is important to remember if everyone in your life seems one way or nobody ever meets your expectations.

Summary

People don't live forever, and relationships don't last forever. Being willing to love deeply despite the costs to us when we lose our loved ones is a powerful gift to cultivate. We do not always know when relationships will end, but when we do, we should reflect on the importance and significance of the relationship with the other person. Relationships require effort and time to maintain. While some friendships seem easier than others, regular connection is important. We have to be willing to check in with ourselves—our feelings, biases, fears, and anxieties—as we are in relationships with others. We have to cultivate the ability to be open and honest and to risk rejection if we want to discern which relationships have the potential for depth and meaning. To connect well, we need to have clear expectations, a range of emotional awareness, clear and open communication, the ability to mend the breaks (or potential breaks) in a relationship, and the willingness to make things right. The potential for any relationship to be transformational is more about the quality of the connection than the amount of time we spend together. If we are blessed, we will have two to three people in our lives with whom we can be genuine. If we are doubly blessed, these will be friends who transcend time and distance—friends with whom connection is easy and seemingly automatic. Establishing such friends involves practicing the skills outlined in this book and cultivating your emotional health. I pray for you the joy and peace that comes from deep and meaningful connections with friends.

Bibliography

"Confront." *Dictionary.com.* https://www.dictionary.com/browse/confront.

Dodd, Chip. 2015. *Voice of the Heart.* 2nd edition. Nashville: Sage Hill, LLC.

Franco, Marissa G. 2022. *Platonic: How Understanding Your Attachment Style Can Help You Make and Keep Friends.* New York: Putnam.

Friedman, Edwin H. 1985. *Generation to Generation: Family Process in Church and Synagogue.* New York: Guilford Press.

———. 1990. *Friedman's Fables.* New York: Guilford Press.

Gibson, Lindsay C. 2015. *Adult Children of Emotionally Immature Parents: How to Heal from Distant, Rejecting, or Self-Involved Parents.* Oakland: New Harbinger Publications.

Godwin, Alan. 2008. *How to Solve Your People Problems: Dealing with Your Difficult Relationships.* Brentwood, TN: Alan Godwin with Rosenbaum & Associates Literary Agency.

Lydon, John E., David W. Jamieson, and John G. Holmes. 1997. "The Meaning of Social Interactions in the Transition from Acquaintanceship to Friendship." *Journal of Personality & Social Psychology.* 536–48.

Keene, Frederick W. 2010. "Structures of Forgiveness in the New Testament." In *Violence Against Women and Children: A Christian Theological Sourcebook,* ed. Carol J. Admas and Marie Fortune,

121–34. London: Continuum. https://www.faithtrustinstitute.org/resources/articles/Structures-of-Forgiveness.pdf.

Kluft, Richard P. 1993. "The Initial Stages of Psychotherapy in the Treatment of Multiple Personality Disorder." *Dissociation* (June/September): 145–60.

Kotin, Joel. 1995. *Getting Started: An Introduction to Dynamic Psychotherapy*. Lanham, MD: Jason Aronson, Inc.

Lambert, M. J., and D. E. Barley. 2001. "Research summary on the therapeutic relationship and psychotherapy outcome." *Psychotherapy: Theory, Research, Practice, Training* 38/4. 357–61.

Miller, William. 1981. *Make Friends with Your Shadow: How to Accept and Use Positively the Negative Side of Your Personality*. Minneapolis: Augsburg.

Nouwen, Henri. 2004. *Out of Solitude: Three Meditations on the Christian Life*. Notre Dame, IN: Ave Maria Press.

Savage, John. 1996. *Listening & Caring Skills: A Guide for Groups & Leaders*. Nashville: Abingdon Press.

Scriven, Joseph, and Charles Crozat. 1885. "What A Friend We Have in Jesus."

www.ingramcontent.com/pod-product-compliance
Lightning Source LLC
Chambersburg PA
CBHW062106080426
42734CB00012B/2769